Stonework

Stonework

Alan & Gill Bridgewater

Voyageur Press

Printed in Malaysia

04 05 06 07 08 5 4 3 2 1

Library of Congress Cataloging-in-Publication Data available

ISBN 0-89658-041-5

Distributed in Canada by Raincoast Books, 9050 Shaughnessy Street, Vancouver, B.C. V6P 6E5

Published by Voyageur Press, Inc.
123 North Second Street, P.O. Box 338, Stillwater, MN 55082 U.S.A.
651-430-2210, fax 651-430-2211
books@voyageurpress.com
www.voyageurpress.com

First published in the United Kingdom by New Holland Publishers (UK) Ltd

Educators, fundraisers, premium and gift buyers, publicists, and marketing managers: Looking for creative products and new sales ideas? Voyageur Press books are available at special discounts when purchased in quantities, and special editions can be created to your specifications. For details contact the marketing department at 800-888-9653.

Legal Notice
The information in this book is true and complete to the best of our knowledge. All recommendations are made without guarantee on the part of the author and publisher. The author and publisher disclaim any liability for damage or injury resulting from the use of this information.

Editorial Direction: Rosemary Wilkinson
Project Editor: Clare Sayer
Production: Hazel Kirkman
Designed and created for New Holland by AG&G Books   Project design: AG&G Books
Project construction: AG&G Books and John Heming   Planting and props: AG&G Books and Vana Haggerty
Photography: AG&G Books and Ian Parsons   Illustrator: Gill Bridgewater
Editor: Fiona Corbridge   Designer: Glyn Bridgewater

Conversion chart

To convert metric measurements to imperial measurements, simply multiply the metric figure by the relevant number shown in the chart to the right. Bear in mind that conversions will not necessarily work out exactly, and you will need to round the figure up or down slightly. (Do not use a combination of metric and imperial measurements—for accuracy, always follow only one system.)

To convert	Multiply by
millimeters to inches	0.0394
meters to feet	3.28
meters to yards	1.093
sq. millimeters to sq. inches	0.00155
sq. meters to sq. feet	10.76
sq. meters to sq. yards	1.195
cu. meters to cu. feet	35.31
cu. meters to cu. yards	1.308
grams to pounds	0.0022
kilograms to pounds	2.2046
liters to gallons	0.22

Contents

Traditional
rock garden
26

Celtic-patterned
walkway
30

Japanese
suiseki stone
34

Old English
random paving
38

Serpentine
walkway
42

Earth-and-stone
retaining wall
46

Japanese
rock garden
50

Stone and
brick walkway
54

Plinth and
slab table
58

Boulder and
coping wall
62

Inlay
block steps
66

Stone
planter
70

Bench with
arch detail
76

Crazy-paving
steps
82

Roman
arch shrine
88

Introduction

When we first entered the Cornish village that encompassed the cottage we eventually bought, we were amazed. Everything was built from local stone, from the houses, roofs, garden walls, and gateposts to the harbor walls, steps, sidewalks, roads, walkways, and the slab in the butcher's shop. The scale of the more monumental structures, such as bridges and the giant battlements around the harbor, was naturally impressive; however, perhaps more than anything else, we were inspired by some of the more modest constructions in the yards—the low walls, the pretty arched seats, and the little flights of steps that meandered down to the water. From that moment on, we were captivated and inspired by the art and craft of stonework.

A brief history

If you could go back to the most primitive cave dwelling, you would find examples of stonework. Although some structures were no more than heaps of stone—to contain a fire, or to form a working surface—they still involved complex mind–eye–hand procedures of selecting and placing stones. And once people had learned these skills, they graduated to creating walls, lintels, arches, houses, and buildings on a much grander scale, such as pyramids and cathedrals.

This dry-stone wall in a field in Ley, India, was constructed using a mixture of large boulders and small cobblestones.

Be inspired

Stonework is an exciting craft: once you have tried it, you will see the world with fresh eyes. Stone walkways, patios, walls, and buildings will fascinate you by showing what is possible when one stone is carefully placed next to another. Take the inspiration back home and translate it into items that will enrich and beautify your garden, giving you many hours of pleasure in the process.

Best of luck

Alan & Gill

This attractive rock garden features a waterfall and pool. The large size of the rocks makes this a dramatic, natural-looking arrangement.

Health and safety

Many stoneworking procedures are potentially dangerous, so before starting work on the projects, check through the following list:

✔ Make sure that you are fit and strong enough for the task ahead of you. If you have doubts, ask your doctor for specific advice.

✔ When you are lifting large lumps of stone from ground level, minimize the risk of back strain by bending your knees, hugging the stone close to your body, and keeping the spine upright.

✔ If a slab of stone looks too heavy to lift on your own, ask others to help. Don't risk injury.

✔ Wear gloves, a dust-mask, and goggles when you are handling cement and lime, or when cutting stone with a hammer and chisel.

✔ Never operate machinery, such as a power drill, or attempt a difficult lifting or maneuvering task if you are overtired or using medication.

✔ Keep a first-aid kit and telephone within easy reach.

Part 1
Techniques

Designing and planning

The secret of good stonework lies in the detail. If you are patient and prepared to spend time thinking through the whole operation involved in a project—from measuring the site and making drawings, to ordering and buying stone, to considering how a seemingly immovable stone can be moved—then not only will you enjoy this book, but your garden will be magically transformed.

Looking at your outdoor space

Assessing your garden

Wander through your garden and observe how the position of the sun—the intensity of the light, and the depth of the shade—changes the mood of the space. Consider the possibilities. Could you blur the difference between indoor and outdoor space by constructing a stone patio right next to the house? Or change the way the garden is used by running a walkway in a new direction? Or encourage a different use of the space by building walls, tables, and benches? There are many exciting alternatives.

Style considerations

Just as you style your interior decor—it might be modern, ethnic, or period, for example—you need to do the same for your outdoor space. Do you simply want it to mirror the character of your indoor space? Or do you want it to be an adventurous reflection of nature?

A quiet, shaded area might be the perfect place for a Japanese-style rock garden

Perhaps a new walkway will encourage you to use more of your outdoor space

A raised planter may be ideal for adding a focal point to a dull area of garden

A patio provides a suitable foundation for other stonework projects, such as a planter or sculpture

Think about the style of a patio area, as well as its size and shape

Whatever the size, shape, and style of your outdoor space, there are likely to be areas that you wish to improve. A patio may be essential, or you may want to build a dramatic stonework sculpture. Sketch out the possibilities on a plan of your garden.

Design

Deciding what to build

Once you have considered your outdoor space in terms of sunlight, mood, and style, you can immerse yourself in the exciting business of deciding just what you want to build. The best way to proceed is to tackle the infrastructure first, then take it from there. So if, for example, your garden lacks walkways and paving, perhaps now is the time to do something about it. Then again, if you have always had an urge to build an arch or a wall, indulge in your dream.

Form and function

In many ways, it is true to say that form follows function—in the sense that you need to ensure that a bench is comfortable before you start to worry about the designer curlicues. However, don't let that stop you using your imagination. For example, if you like our Roman Arch Shrine (see page 88), but would prefer to build a whole row of shrines the full length of the garden, go ahead.

Choosing stone

Any stonework project has certain essential requirements—such as for thin slabs of stone or square blocks—but apart from

at, various materials are suitable. To see
hat is available, visit suppliers who sell
one, salvaged stone, and concrete stone,
ch as stone yards and home centers.

rawing your designs

nce you have looked at your garden,
d considered your needs in terms of
esign, size, function, stone supply, and
sts, turn to the projects. If you do not
e exactly what you are looking for,
ketch out your ideas and then work out
ow a project might be modified. Draw
ur design to a rough scale, complete
ith the number of courses of stone. A
od way of planning out the building
ages is to divide the project into lay-
rs—the foundation slab, the first course
f stone, the next course, and so on—
en draw the layers on paper. This will
ot only help clarify the order of work,
ut it will also reveal potential problems.

is helpful to create a picture scrapbook
f stone structures, augmented by garden
phemera, such as planters, that appeal to
ou. Use it for ideas and inspiration when
anning a stonework design.

Planning

irst steps

lan out the logistics of the project. First,
ecide where all the materials are going
be stored. If you are having stone
elivered, ask if it will be unloaded on a
allet or whether you will be expected to
elp unload it by hand. Sometimes sand
nd gravel are delivered in huge bags and
nloaded with a winch, so check that
here is an adequate accessible space for
hem to be stored. Where are you going
put the removed turf and waste soil?

Will the building procedures get in
he way of other activities of the house-
old, such as getting the car out or chil-
ren playing? Will you require help when
comes to mixing concrete or moving
tone? Will you need to cover the project

with a plastic sheet if it starts to rain? Try
to visualize every eventuality and forestall
potential problems.

Permission and safety

Check with your local building authority
that there are no planning restrictions
governing the type of structure you are
intending to build. Permits are often necessary for large renovations, but evern a
small job, such as building a low wall
around a patio, may require a permit.

For safety's sake, dress properly for
the task ahead. You must protect your
hands with strong gloves and your feet
with heavy boots. Make sure that children are out of harm's way when it comes
to lifting heavy stones and slabs.

Planning checklist

✔ Is there a stone quarry in your
area? This is likely to be the most
economical source of materials.

✔ Is there access to your back yard?
If the stone is unloaded in your
driveway, or front yard, will it cause
problems or pose a danger?

✔ How are you going to move the
stone to the site? Can you do it,
or do you need friends to help?

✔ Is your garden reasonably level,
with walkways wide enough for
a wheelbarrow? Or does it have
soft, spring lawns and very
few walkways—if so, what
arrangements do you need to
make to move the materials?

Materials

For the projects in this book, all you need to know about the primary materials—stone and sand—are their common names, color, and working characteristics. Once you know that sandstone splits into easy-to-work slices, and salvaged roof slate is good when you want to build a structure in thin courses, the rest is easy.

Stone, concrete, and mortar

Stone shape and color

All the projects involve breaking stone with a chisel (instead of using an angle grinder), so the two best types of stone to use are sandstone, which breaks into thin sheets, and limestone, which breaks into squarish blocks. Explain your needs to the supplier, see what stone is available, check its working characteristics, then look for pieces in the color of your choice.

Natural stone versus concrete pavers

The color and texture of natural stone cannot be beaten; however, it is more expensive than concrete pavers that are made to imitate stone. We prefer to use natural stone for walls and arrangements, and concrete pavers when we need large, square-cut slabs or pavers. We did use concrete pavers for walling in the Earth-and-Stone Border Wall (see page 46), but this is with the hope that once you have tried your hand with pavers, you will have the confidence to build a more complex wall project using natural stone.

Other materials

Clean well-graded mortar sand is usually used for making smooth mortar, and clean, coarser sand for making concrete and coarse-textured mortar. However, we used well-graded masonry sand for most of the mortar mixes, and coarser sand to form the aggregate (a mixture of sand and gravel) when making concrete. This way of working enables you to buy the sand in bulk. Gravel and crushed stone are used both as decorative spreads and as a base-layer to create a drainage bed.

Buying stone

Decide on the color and character of stone required for the project, then visit a quarry or stone yard and buy the stone as seen. Most stone is sold by the square yard or cubic yard. Pick out the pieces and spread them on the ground to fill a square yard—this allows you to see how the pieces relate to each other for the purposes of the project. Never buy stone without looking at it first.

Opposite page: A selection of materials suitable for making the projects in this book (concrete products are available at building supply stores):
1 Concrete paver block, 2 Concrete block, 3 Concrete paver rope-top edging, 4 Corner post 5 Celtic pattern paver and square paver, 6 Clay roof tile, 7 Limestone, 8 Sandstone, 9 Brick, 10 Roof slate, 11 Flagstone, 12 Medium-sized cobblestone, 13 Concrete paver, 14 Sandstone, 15 Statue, 16 Rock, 17 Crushed stone, 18 Radius paving, 19 Gravel, 20 Feature stone, 21 Large concrete paver, 22 Small concrete paver

Concrete and mortar mixes

Mortar and concrete both contain aggregates, cement, and water, but are made according to different recipes. Most stoneworkers have their own favorites. Some people make mortar using 1 part cement, 5 parts sand, and 1 part lime; others use 1 part cement, 6 parts well-graded mortar sand, and don't bother with the lime. The quantities we give in the projects are generous and allow for wastage. We use the following mixes:

- Concrete for general foundations: 1 part Portland cement to 5 parts aggregate (ranging from small stones down to coarse sand).

- Concrete for paths: 1 part Portland cement to 4 parts aggregate.

- Mortar for a general mix: 1 part Portland cement to 4 parts well-graded mortar sand.

- Mortar for a smooth, strong mix: 1 part Portland cement, 1 part lime, and 3–4 parts well-graded mortar sand.

Tools

Tools are one of the main keys to successful stonework. Although the best tools are no substitute for enthusiasm and determination, carefully chosen, top-quality tools will ensure that each and every task is accomplished with minimum effort and maximum efficiency, in the shortest possible time. However, it is fine to begin by using existing tools for the projects—just buy new ones if and when the need arises.

Choosing and using the correct tools

Measuring and marking

You will need a flexible tape measure and a straightedge for measuring the site, a rule for taking smaller measurements within the project, pegs and string for setting out the shape of the project on the ground, a spirit level to check that the project is both vertically and horizontally level, and a piece of chalk for drawing registration marks. It will make your life easier if you have two flexible tape measures—a small, steel one for making measurements up to 10 feet, and a large, wipe-clean fibreglass tape for measuring over longer distances in the yard.

Moving soil

Get yourself a spade for slicing into grass and for digging holes, and a fork for picking up turf. To move soil from one spot to another, you need a shovel, a wheelbarrow, and one or more buckets. If you are moving a lot of soil, it is a good idea to obtain a rake for spreading out the soil on the site.

Cutting and breaking stone

Apart from strong gloves to safeguard your hands and stout boots to protect your feet, you will require a sledgehammer for compacting the bottom gravel level, a club hammer and brick chisel for cutting and splitting stone, and a bricklayer's hammer for the more precise task of cutting and pecking small pieces of stone to shape. An old piece of carpet is a good surface to work on. For cleaning the stone and tidying up the site at the end of work, have a wire brush, broom, and a small hand brush at hand. If you are prone to suffer from aches and pains, especially in your knees, it is a good idea to use an old cushion or padded kneeling mat to kneel on while you work.

Mixing concrete and mortar

You will need a shovel for moving the sand, cement, and aggregate, a bucket for carrying water and small amounts of the concrete or mortar mixture, and a wheelbarrow for moving large amounts of the mixture around the yard. If you discover that you really enjoy working with stone and intend to do a lot of it, a small electric mixer will make the task of mixing concrete and mortar a lot easier. Always wash mortar and concrete off tools as soon as you have finished working, especially in hot weather when the mixtures are liable to harden quickly.

Laying stone

Once the concrete and mortar have been moved to the site, you must have a brick trowel (a large trowel) for handling large amounts of mortar, and a pointing trowel (a small trowel) for tidying up the joints and making good. We also use the brick trowel to carry the mortar when we are using the pointing trowel to do the pointing. When the stone is nicely bedded on the mortar, it is tapped into place with a club hammer or a rubber malle[t]. The measurements and levels ar[e] checked to make sure that they are co[r]rect. Finally, about an hour after th[e] stone has been laid, when the mortar ha[s] started to cure, the excess mortar [is] removed with a trowel.

General tasks

At various points along the way, we use [a] claw hammer for banging in and pullin[g] out nails, a crosscut saw for sizing length[s] of wood, a portable brace in conjunctio[n] with drill bits for drilling holes and [a] screwdriver bit for driving in screws, an[d] a utility knife to cut string and plast[ic] sheet. We use all types of odd-shape[d] pieces of plywood and board for protec[t]ing the site and as workboards to ho[ld] piles of mortar. If you value your existin[g] lawn, start the project by surrounding th[e] site with workboards so that the grass [is] covered and safeguarded from damage b[y] feet, wheelbarrows, and tools.

Caution
Power tools

Electricity, early-morning dew, buckets of water, and wet hands are a potentially dangerous combination. If you use a powe[r] drill instead of a portable brace, or you use an electric cement mixer, make sure that you use them in conjunction with a ground fault circuit interrupter (GFCI), which will protect you against potential electric shock[.]

A basic tool kit

For making the projects in this book, you will need the tools shown below. All of these can be bought from home centers or a local hardware store. The angle grinder is optional—it is comparatively expensive and not essential for the projects. However, if you are planning to do a lot of stonework projects in the future that involve cutting stone, it may be a worthwhile investment. Likewise, an electric cement mixer (not illustrated) may also be useful.

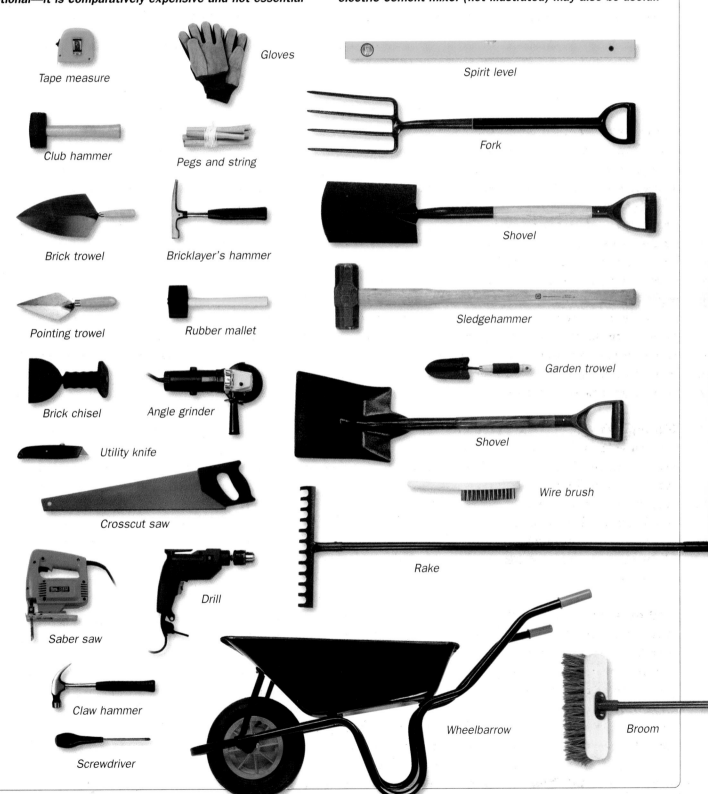

Tape measure

Gloves

Spirit level

Club hammer

Pegs and string

Fork

Brick trowel

Bricklayer's hammer

Shovel

Pointing trowel

Rubber mallet

Sledgehammer

Brick chisel

Angle grinder

Garden trowel

Shovel

Utility knife

Wire brush

Crosscut saw

Rake

Saber saw

Drill

Claw hammer

Wheelbarrow

Broom

Screwdriver

Basic techniques

Once you have mastered the basic techniques, working with stone is a wonderfully therapeutic experience. After a day or so of practicing the basic techniques, such as cutting stone and mixing mortar, you will be able to tackle any of the projects in this book. And after a weekend of putting your skills into practice, you will see a fascinating structure emerge from a heap of stone and a pile of sand.

When you have chosen your site and made sure that it is right for the project, measure out the area needed and mark it with pegs and string. If the foundation is square or rectangular, check that corners are at right angles by making sure that the two diagonal measurements are identical. The two-peg technique at the corners (see photo on the right) not only allows you to set out the shape without cutting the string, but also to dig the trench without the pegs getting in the way. Use a natural-fiber string that is less likely to twist and knot itself.

Marking out

Make sure the strings cross at right angles

You can choose to wet the string prior to use so that it shrinks and tightens on the pegs

Use pegs and string to mark out the size and shape of a site. Double-check your measurements every step of the way.

Preparing a foundation

Rock the ends of the wooden screed against the top edge of the form

You may need to add or remove concrete to achieve the correct level

Use a frame of wood (form) set level in the ground to establish the area for the concrete slab. Fill the form with concrete and tamp and scrape it level.

Building a form

With the shape of the foundation marked with pegs and string, dig the soil to the required depth. If the soil drains poorly or you live in an area subject to ground heave due to frost, dig deeper to include a 4-inch bed of gravel or crushed stone. In mild areas where the ground is firm and dry, gravel is not needed, but if you have clay or other difficult-to-grade soil, then use a 2- to 3-inch gravel bed.

Using the form boards and form pegs, build a frame within the recess. Bang two pegs in the ground, set one board level against the pegs, and screw it in place. Position the second board against the first and secure it with pegs, then continue until the frame is complete. Use the spirit level to check that the top edge of the frame is level. If it is necessary to hit the frame slightly to adjust the level, remove the spirit level first.

Laying the concrete slab

When the form has been built, spread the drainage material—gravel or crushed stone—within the frame and use the sledgehammer to tamp it down. Continue until you have a firm, compact base.

Starting from one end of the form, pour concrete over the base. Spread it roughly with the shovel, and use a length of wood to tamp it level with the top of the form. The general rule with concrete is the dryer the mix, the stronger the finished concrete slab.

Cutting stone

Using a brick chisel

A brick chisel and club hammer are used to break stones in two. Mark the line of cut with a straightedge and a piece of chalk. Wear gloves to guard your hands and goggles to protect your eyes. Keep children and pets out of the way, because of the danger of flying shards of stone. Place the stone on a block of wood, a pad of old carpet, or even a pile of sand, set the brick chisel on the line, and give it a series of taps with the club hammer. Repeat this procedure on both sides of

the stone to score a line. Now increase the force of the blow until the stone breaks in two. Don't be tempted to try and break the stone with a single, crashing blow—it rarely works!

Using a bricklayer's hammer

A bricklayer's hammer is used to trim stones to shape. Hold the stone firmly in one hand, so that the edge to be trimmed is farthest away from you. Take the bricklayer's hammer and use the chisel end of the head to chip the edge into shape.

Use a brick chisel and a club hammer to cut (break) pieces of stone. Hold the chisel upright and hit it several times.

Building

Laying courses of stone

Mix the mortar to a smooth, buttery consistency, so that it is firm without being watery. Dampen the pile of stones. Trowel mortar on the foundation slab and set the first stone in place. Butter the end of the next stone with mortar and bed it into the mortar on the slab, with its end butted firmly against the first stone. When you have a line of stones, take a club hammer or rubber mallet and gently tap the stones into line. Don't fuss around with the mortar that oozes out, other than to gather it up and throw it back on

the pile. Make sure that bits of hard mortar and stone do not get thrown back into the mortar heap.

Leveling the courses

When you have put down a group of stones, it is necessary to check and adjust the vertical and horizontal levels. Stand back and try to identify problems, then put a length of wood on the stones, and tap it with the hammer until the offending stones fall into line. Place the spirit level against the wood to take a reading, then make further adjustments if needed.

When you are laying courses of stones, remember to stagger the joints and check each course is level before proceeding.

Filling joints

Filling joints

When you have finished a section of wall, the cavities will need to be filled or pointed. Use the small pointing trowel to spread a ³⁄₈-inch layer of buttery mortar over the back of the large brick trowel. Using the large trowel as your palette and the small trowel like a spatula, slice through the mortar to reveal a straight edge, then pick up a ³⁄₈-inch-wide strip on the back edge of the small trowel (so that you have a square-section worm) and wipe it into the cavity. Follow the procedure on all open joints. This is a

skill that needs to be practiced. Hold the trowels in the way that is most comfortable for you, and you will be more likely to get good results.

Pointing and raking joints

You can either wait until the mortar is firm, then use the trowel to tool it to a smooth, shaped finish, or you can wait until the mortar is hard and rake out the joints to reveal the edges of the stone. Most projects in this book favor the raking option. Do not be tempted to rake out mortar while it is still soft.

After filling crazy-paving joints with mortar, use a pointing trowel to shape the mortar into an angled or slightly peaked finish.

Walkways, steps, and patios

Walkways, steps, and patios are functionally desirable in that they provide dry, level areas enabling us to move around the garden in comfort. They are also visually desirable—who can resist exploring a walkway that curves out of sight, or climbing steps that lead up a slope, or sitting on a shaded patio? You can visit parks, gardens, and stately homes to get an idea of possibilities varying from the simple to the grandiose.

Constructing walkways

Designing and planning

Study the site and decide on the route and the type of walkway, including the depth and structure of the foundation, and the type of surface material and edging required. Use the tape measure, pegs, and string to mark out the route on the ground. Make sure that the layout does not upset the balance of the garden.

Building

Dig out the soil to the required depth, spread the gravel over the site, and top it with your chosen surface—sand, aggregate, or concrete. If the ground is soft and/or wet, a firmer foundation is needed, so dig out the soil to a greater depth, increase the thickness of the gravel bed, and use concrete instead sand or aggregate. Bed the stone, pavers, or slabs on generous blobs of mortar. Dig a trench and bed the edging in mortar. Finally, fill the joints with sand or mortar.

This beautifully crafted, natural-looking walkway is built from Gloucestershire stone. The stones are set on edge (a traditional technique) in a mixture of clay and crushed stone. The walkway may be a little bumpy to walk on, but would look good in a traditional garden. Curved or undulating paths can also be built using the same technique.

INSPIRATIONS

A mixture of brick pavers and stone lends itself to rectangular layouts.

The precise shapes of molded concrete slabs allow you to create complex patterns.

Natural stone steps edged by rock garden stones are ideal for a fairly informal garden.

Constructing steps

Designing and planning

Decide on the number and height of the risers, and the depth of the treads. Measure the average thickness of the stone you intend to use to determine how many courses you need for each riser.

Building

Use pegs and string to set out the foundation, then dig to the required depth, set the form in the recess and fill it with gravel and concrete. Build the first riser and side walls and back-fill with gravel. Set the first tread in place. Build subsequent steps in the same way.

These rock garden steps are like stepping stones and seem to be part of the landscape. More formal steps needs careful planning with a tape measure, length of wood, and spirit level.

Constructing a patio

This blue-gray patio is made of random pieces of slate laid as crazy paving. It includes a circular feature made of stones set on edge in a radiating pattern, looking like a fossilized ammonite.

Designing and planning

Use the tape measure, string and pegs to scribe the shape of the patio on the ground. If you are using concrete pavers, do your best to make sure that the patio is made up from a number of whole units, so that you don't have to cut slabs.

Building

Dig the foundation to the required depth and set the form in place. Check the levels and adjust the form so that there is a very slight fall to one side, so the patio will shed surface water. Spread the gravel bed and sand, aggregate, or concrete. Bed the surface material on mortar.

Recessed steps, together with symmetrical decorative urns, give a classical feel to an area.

A patio and walkway made of stone pavers, stepping stones, cobblestones, and gravel.

A circular patio and a radiating design attract attention and so become a focal point.

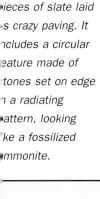

Walls and other structures

Walls, containers, pedestals, and other freestanding structures are usually built from courses of stone, and extra care is needed to build strong, safe structures that will not fall down. Once completed, there is a good chance that they will still be in existence in a hundred years' time. Walls are capable of making a powerful statement in your garden, with aesthetic possibilities, as well as practical advantages.

Constructing walls

Designing and planning

Decide where you want the wall. Do you want a dry-stone wall or are you going to use mortar? Do you want an easy-to-build low wall (such as a three-course wall across the corner of the garden), or a more complex freestanding structure that needs a substantial foundation?

Once you have decided on the height, form, and construction, sit down with a pencil and paper and work out the quantities of stone, sand and cement.

Building

Use a tape measure, pegs, and string to establish the shape of the foundation trench. Dig the trench, half-fill it with gravel, and top it with concrete. Select stone for the first few courses and have a dry run to test placement. Then either lay the stones with mud if it is an earth-and-stone wall (see Earth-and-Stone Retaining Wall on page 46), or use mortar.

This dry-stone wall in Wales is made from chunky slabs of slate. Note how the builder has selected and placed the stones to create a strong and attractive pattern.

INSPIRATIONS

Mixed materials and built-in shelves provide a beautiful backdrop for container plants.

This stone wall with decorative coping (top pieces) could make a good boundary wall in a yard.

A seating area can be achieved by incorporating large, outward-extending slabs into the wall.

Constructing containers

This container is made from a single piece of found stone. Not everyone is lucky enough to find a piece of naturally hollowed stone such as this, but it is possible to make your own using tufa (see the Japanese Suiseki stone on page 34).

Designing and planning

Establish the shape, height, and composition of the container. Decide whether it needs a foundation, such as a slab, a trench full of gravel, or a trench with gravel and concrete, then use the tape measure, pegs, and string to mark the shape of the foundation on the ground.

Building

Once the foundation is in place, take your chosen stone and set out the first two or three courses dry, choosing the best possible stones for the corners. Secure the courses in place with mortar.

Constructing columns and pedestals

Designing, planning, and building

Columns and pedestals are just small containers with the centers filled in, so you can follow the same designing, planing, and building procedures already described. Build with care and attention, especially when it comes to checking the horizontal and vertical levels, because any inaccuracies are swiftly accentuated and highlighted by the modest size of the structure. Remember that there is always a correlation between the height of the structure and the size of the foundation. If you want to build a tall structure (more than 3 feet high) the foundation needs to be proportionally wider.

As an alternative to building a pedestal from a lot of small pieces of stone, you can search around for large, solid pieces. Here, disc-shaped stones form striking pedestals for displaying plant containers or ornaments.

Decorative stone containers, full of plants, add interest and warmth to a plain paved area.

A bold stone structure is sometimes all that is needed to decorate your garden.

A two-tier pedestal for displaying plants could also form a retaining wall.

Rock gardens and other stone arrangements

Rock gardens are built in direct imitation of nature; other garden stone arrangements are often built as a contrast or may even have a symbolic purpose, containing spheres, cones, or Japanese lanterns, for example Examine stones in nature, art, and architecture, then draw inspiration from your observations.

Constructing a rock garden

This striking rock garden and waterfall has large rocks that have been positioned in imitation of a natural rocky slope. (If you want to make a rock garden without huge rocks, see the Traditional Rockery project on page 26, which uses thin layers of stone instead.)

Designing and planning

To give you ideas for constructing a natural-looking rock garden, think about the beaches and mountains you have visited. Use a tape measure, pegs, and string to map the shape of the rock garden on the ground. Remember that if you are going to use huge rocks, you have to find some way of getting them to the site. I may be easier to group small rocks, which are relatively easy to move, so that they look like large outcrops.

Building

Clear the site of all weeds and cover i with shale, gravel, or crushed stone Arrange the rocks in groups or stacks and tilt them so that they rear up at a angle. Create small pockets of rich soil al over the site for filling with rock garden plants. Cover a good proportion of th rocks and soil with your chosen grit gravel, or crushed shell.

INSPIRATIONS

A miniature version of a stony landscape will blend well into almost any small garden.

This arrangement of bold plants bordered by large rocks looks like a natural outcrop.

A design using ground-covering stone, plants, and rocks can mimic a river and its banks.

Japanese-style arrangements

Designing and building

For the Japanese, the art of rock arrangement is based on using a small number of stones to create a blend of nature and symbolism, and each and every stone that plays a part needs to be chosen with great care. When creating your own version try, if possible, to use timeworn stones covered in moss and lichen, which impart subtle color, shape, and character to the arrangement.

Sculptures and other found objects

Designing and building

The wonderful thing about using stone sculptures and found stones is that you can follow your intuition and create an arrangement that is uniquely your own. If you like stone frogs or gnomes, or have a passion for collecting pebbles, you are halfway to having a very special rock garden. Set aside a corner—perhaps an area ringed with rocks—then simply set out your sculptures and found stones, allowing the arrangement to evolve.

A beautifully built cone, which may not be particularly useful, is a great piece of sculpture for the garden. Any bold shape like this will probably dominate a small garden, so make sure you really want one.

This traditional Japanese design uses bamboo to deliver water to a stone basin.

A simple walkway design is remarkably powerful when placed in stark surroundings.

A "river" of randomly shaped stones forms an attractive walkway and is easy to build.

Part 2

Projects

Traditional rock garden

Anyone who has a natural outcrop of rock in the garden has the perfect place for planting beautiful "alpines" (high-mountain plants) and plants with a dwarf or trailing habit. You can create the same effect by building a rock garden with a lot of nooks and crannies for the plants. The great thing about this project is that the rock garden is made from small, easy-to-handle stones, which can be transported in your car without difficulty.

★
Easy

Making time
One weekend
One day for clearing the site and setting the rocks in place, and one day for planting

Considering the design

It would be nice if you could wave a magic wand and conjure up a series of dramatic monolithic rocks in your garden. However, the expense, physical challenge, and access difficulties involved in moving large single rocks into an established garden make most people shy away from the prospect. It's much easier to build a rock garden from small, manageable rocks, and we have designed the project with this in mind.

The slices of rock are stacked like slices of bread and arranged to resemble the tip of a sloping outcrop of stone breaking through the ground. Note how the groups of stones are placed in steps, and the line of steps both rears up and angles across the bed. The borders of the rock garden are defined by stones set on edge.

Getting started

Walk around your garden and look at the various possible sites. Ideally, you need a site that is gently sloping, well drained, and has no overhanging trees. It should receive plenty of sun, because many rock garden plants prefer these conditions.

You will need

Tools

- ✔ Tape measure
- ✔ Pegs and string
- ✔ Spade, fork, rake, and shovel
- ✔ Wheelbarrow and bucket
- ✔ Club hammer

Materials

For a rock garden 6 ft. 6 in. long and 3 ft. wide

- ✔ Sandstone: about 3 sq. yd. of split sandstone, in the largest sizes that you can manage (rock garden stones)
- ✔ Sandstone: about 2 sq. yd. of split sandstone in random small sizes (coping edging)
- ✔ Crushed stone: 660 lb. of large-size, well-washed crushed stone
- ✔ Gravel: 220 lb. of well-washed gravel in a color to match the stone
- ✔ Planting mixture: 1 part (110 lb.) topsoil, 1 part (110 lb.) fine grit, gravel or stone chippings, 1 part (110 lb.) leaf mold
- ✔ Rock garden plants (such as sedum, alyssum, aubretia, campanula, cerastium, erigeron, primula, saponaria, sempervivum, saxifrage, thyme; bulbs such as dwarf narcissus, crocus, cyclamen, chionodoxa, and muscari)

Overall dimensions and general notes

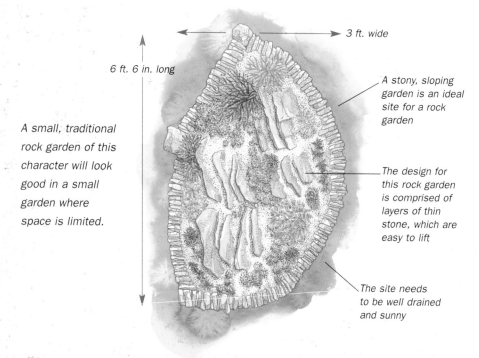

3 ft. wide

6 ft. 6 in. long

A small, traditional rock garden of this character will look good in a small garden where space is limited.

A stony, sloping garden is an ideal site for a rock garden

The design for this rock garden is comprised of layers of thin stone, which are easy to lift

The site needs to be well drained and sunny

Cut-away view of the traditional rock garden

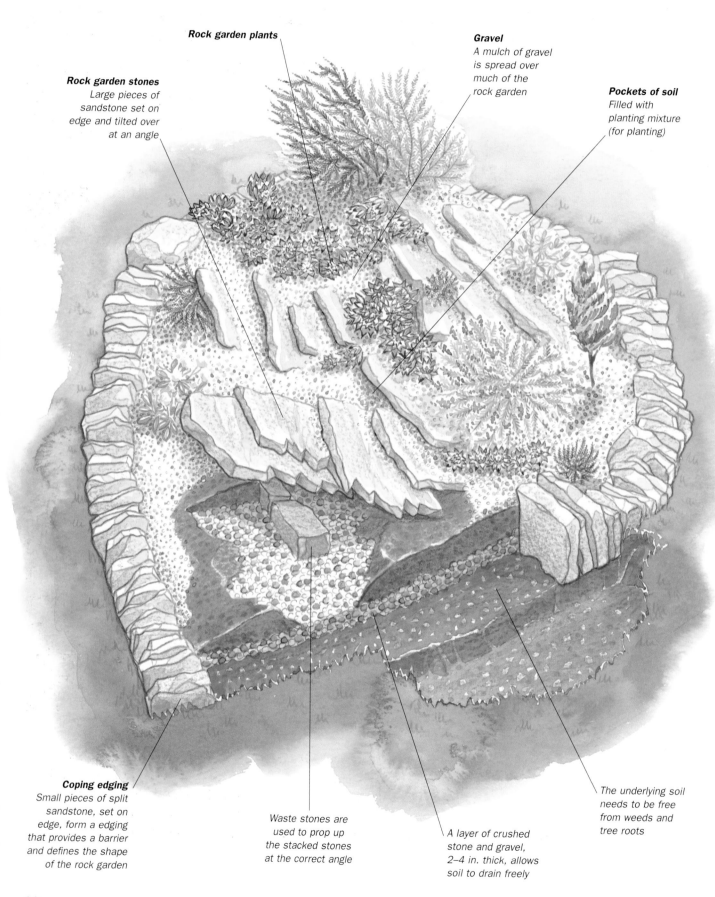

Rock garden plants

Gravel
A mulch of gravel
is spread over
much of the
rock garden

Rock garden stones
Large pieces of
sandstone set on
edge and tilted over
at an angle

Pockets of soil
Filled with
planting mixture
(for planting)

Coping edging
Small pieces of split
sandstone, set on
edge, form a edging
that provides a barrier
and defines the shape
of the rock garden

Waste stones are
used to prop up
the stacked stones
at the correct angle

A layer of crushed
stone and gravel,
2–4 in. thick, allows
soil to drain freely

The underlying soil
needs to be free
from weeds and
tree roots

Making the traditional rock garden

1 Measuring out
Measure out the area for the rock garden, clear the turf and weeds, and define it with a simple coping made from stones set on edge. Dig over the site and increase the drainage by adding a small amount of crushed stones and gravel to the soil.

2 Covering with crushed stone
Rake crushed stone and gravel over the whole site to a depth of about 2–4 in. Tread it into the soil until the entire area feels firm underfoot.

3 Stacking the stone
Stack the split sandstone side by side, in groups of three or four slices. Arrange the leading edges of the stones so that the profiles look natural in relation to each other.

4 Stabilizing the rock garden
Use pieces of waste stone to prop up the stacks of stone so that they all rear up at the same angle. Pack additional crushed stone under the stacks to make them stable and firm.

5 Adding soil
Rake the planting mixture over the whole arrangement and pack it under the stones. Look for natural planting areas, and make sure that they are covered by a generous thickness of soil.

6 Planting
Purchase suitable rock garden plants. Spend time considering the best possible arrangement before you plant them. Water them in, and water regularly until established.

Celtic-patterned walkway

If you enjoy color and Celtic imagery, this walkway will appeal. It is a good, strong, formal walkway that is hardwearing and long-lasting. The imitation standstone flagstones and terracotta trim (both made from concrete) ensure a firm, nonslippery surface. The walkway is made up from three component parts: a basic flagstone, a Celtic knot strip, and a Celtic corner square (used in a central position in the design).

★
Easy

Making time
Two weekends
Two days for laying the concrete, and two days for laying the slabs and finishing details

Considering the design

The pattern consists of a number of repeats, each comprising two flagstones surrounded by three strips and a single corner square. The path is 42 inches wide. The length of the strips allows the slabs to be set in place with an all-round joint width of about ¼ inch.

Getting started

Decide how long you want your path to be. Divide the total length by 24 inches to work out how many repeats you need, then multiply the number of components in the repeat to give you the total amounts of materials required.

Overall dimensions and general notes

24 in. long

42 in. wide

You can change the design to su your needs (the paving strips car run either side of the walkway instead of down the middle or choose strips in another pattern)

This bold, colorful walkway works well in many styles of yards, from minimalist modern spaces to traditional courtyards. The design is only suitable for a straight walkway.

You will need

Tools

✔ Tape measure and straightedge
✔ Pegs and string
✔ Spade, fork, and shovel
✔ Wheelbarrow and bucket
✔ Crosscut saw
✔ Claw hammer
✔ Club hammer
✔ Sledgehammer
✔ Tamping beam: about 5 ft. long, 2⅜ in. wide, and 1⅛ in. thick
✔ Brick trowel
✔ Spirit level

✔ Rubber mallet
✔ Pointing trowel
✔ Soft-bristled brush

Materials

All quantities are per 24 in. of walkway (1 repeat). Walkway is 42 in. wide

✔ Concrete limestone paving slabs: 2 slabs, 18 in. square
✔ Celtic knot terracotta paving strips: 3 strips, 18 in. long, 6 in. wide and 1½ in. thick
✔ Celtic knot terracotta corner square: 1 piece, 6 in. square and 1½ in. thick

✔ Pine lumber: length to suit your walkway, 6 in. wide and ¾ in. thick (form)
✔ Pine lumber: length to suit width of your walkway, 1⅛ in. wide and ¾ in. thick (divider boards, tamping beam, and form pegs)
✔ Gravel or crushed stone: 2 wheelbarrow loads
✔ Concrete: 1 part (30 lb.) Portland cement, 3 parts (90 lb.) aggregate
✔ Mortar: 1 part (22 lb.) Portland cement, 2 parts (44 lb.) well-graded mortar sand
✔ Nails: 2 lb. of 1½-in.-long nails

Cut-away view of the Celtic-pattern walkway

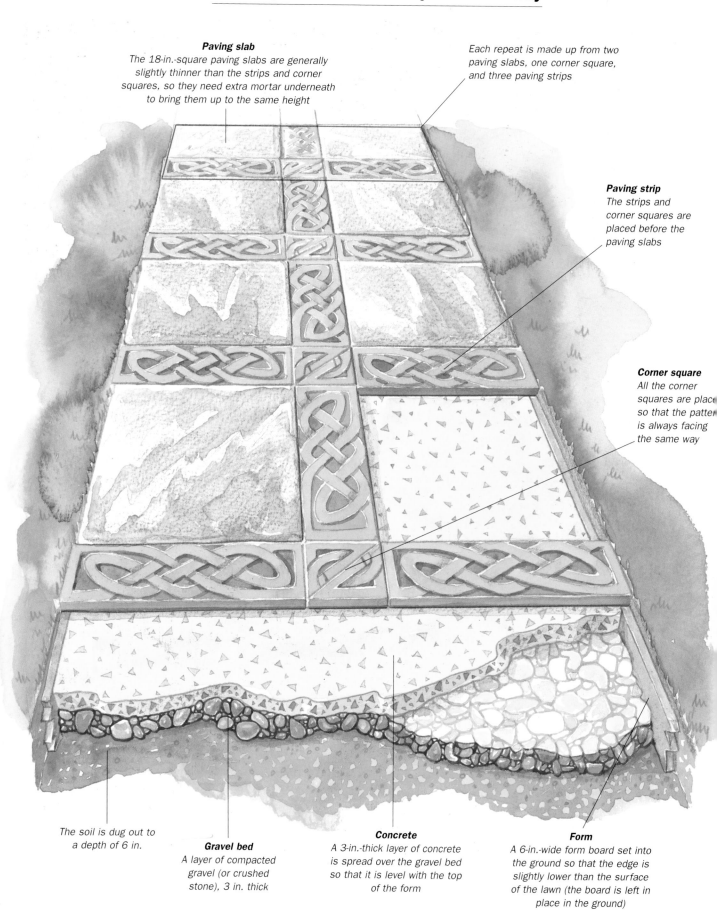

Paving slab
The 18-in.-square paving slabs are generally slightly thinner than the strips and corner squares, so they need extra mortar underneath to bring them up to the same height

Each repeat is made up from two paving slabs, one corner square, and three paving strips

Paving strip
The strips and corner squares are placed before the paving slabs

Corner square
All the corner squares are place so that the patter is always facing the same way

The soil is dug out to a depth of 6 in.

Gravel bed
A layer of compacted gravel (or crushed stone), 3 in. thick

Concrete
A 3-in.-thick layer of concrete is spread over the gravel bed so that it is level with the top of the form

Form
A 6-in.-wide form board set into the ground so that the edge is slightly lower than the surface of the lawn (the board is left in place in the ground)

Making the Celtic-pattern walkway

1 Setting up the form

Mark out the walkway, making it 2 in. wide. Dig out the soil to a depth of 6 in. Put the form boards in the recess, nailing them with the claw hammer and securing them in place with the form pegs. Compact a 3-in. layer of gravel on the walkway.

2 Filling with concrete

Set divider boards every 6–10 ft. across the width of the walkway to allow for expansion of the concrete. Mix the concrete to a thick consistency. Shovel it over the gravel bed, and use the tamping beam to tamp it level with the top edge of the form.

3 Establishing guidelines

Use string to mark out a guideline at one side of the walkway. Placing the paving strips against this, set out another guideline 18 in. in from the side to mark the position of the corner squares in the center of the walkway.

4 Laying the strips

Mix the mortar to a stiff, buttery consistency, and lay the corner squares and paving strips down the center of the walkway. Use the spirit level and rubber mallet to ensure that they are level.

5 Laying the paving slabs

Lay each limestone paving slab by setting five generous, bun-sized blobs of mortar on the walkway. Position the slabs so that they are level with the paving strips. Make sure that the joints are consistently ¼ in. wide.

6 Pointing

Finally, mix a small amount of mortar to a dry, crumbly consistency, and brush and trowel it into the joints. Wait about four hours, then brush all surplus mortar off the walkway.

Japanese suiseki stone

Traditional Japanese gardens make great use of stone for ornamental and symbolic purposes. One such stone is termed a *suiseki*—meaning a large, natural basin. Our suiseki combines Japanese heritage with the very English craft of making stonelike containers from tufa, which is a mixture of moss, sand, and cement. If you like the notion of East meeting West, this project will add oriental tranquillity to your garden.

Making time
One weekend
One day for casting the stone, and one day for arranging the stone and the cobblestones

Overall dimensions and general notes

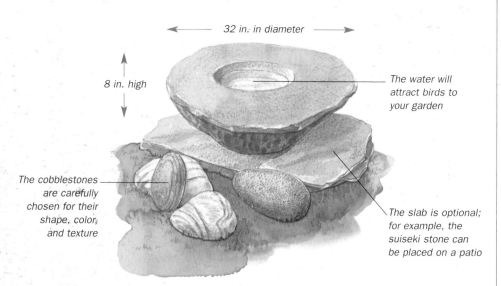

← 32 in. in diameter →

8 in. high

The water will attract birds to your garden

The cobblestones are carefully chosen for their shape, color, and texture

The slab is optional; for example, the suiseki stone can be placed on a patio

The suiseki will look good in slightly wild settings; also in a modern garden or courtyard. It is a traditional element in Japanese gardens, which are famed for their relaxing qualities.

You will need

Tools
- ✔ Workboard: 3 ft. square
- ✔ Wheelbarrow
- ✔ Shovel
- ✔ Bucket
- ✔ Rubber gloves
- ✔ Brick trowel
- ✔ Tape measure and a spirit level
- ✔ Wire snips
- ✔ Paintbrush

Materials
For a suiseki stone 32 in. in diameter and 8 in. high

- ✔ Tufa mix:
  1 part (50 lb.) cement, 1½ parts (75 lb) sphagnum peat, 1½ parts (75 lb) perlite
- ✔ Bowl: metal or plastic, 12 in. in diameter at the rim, 6¾ in. in diameter at the base, and 4 in. in height
- ✔ Bar of kitchen soap
- ✔ Wire grid mesh: 1 in. mesh, about 16 in. square
- ✔ Mortar: 1 part (5 lb.) Portland cement, 3 parts (15 lb.) well-graded mortar sand
- ✔ Varnish: about 4 cupfuls of waterproofing medium
- ✔ Cobblestones for decoration

Considering the design

This is one of the easiest projects in the book—the suiseki stone emerges after a straightforward process, which really only involves pressing the tufa mix over an upturned bowl to create a cast basin. However, the simplicity of its creation belies the finished effect—once the basin is displayed with one or two specimen rocks and stones, and shown off against a subtle backdrop of carefully chosen plants, perhaps in a quiet and protected corner of the yard, it comes into its own as an object of surprising beauty. In a Japanese garden, the suiseki symbolizes the refreshing and purifying aspects of nature, such as dew on a leaf, or water in the cleft of a rock.

The suiseki is about 32 inches wide at the rim and 8 inches tall, and the undercut and textured underside contrasts with the smooth and level top surface.

Getting started

Start searching for a smooth plastic or metal bowl that is wider at the rim than at the base. We used a stainless-steel bowl found in a thrift shop, 12 inches in diameter at the rim, 6¾ inches in diameter at the base, and 4 inches in height.

Cross-section of the Japanese suiseki stone during construction (the stone is upside down)

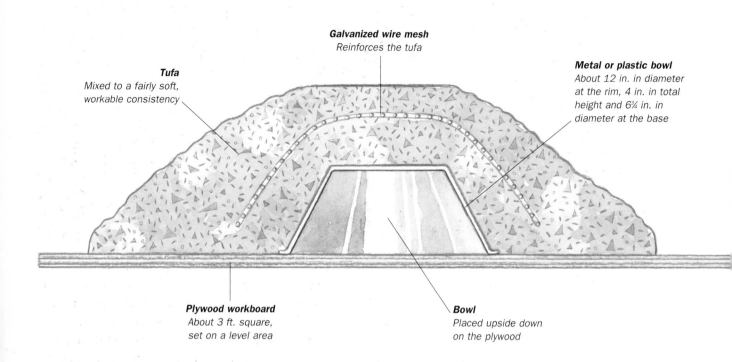

Galvanized wire mesh
Reinforces the tufa

Tufa
*Mixed to a fairly soft,
workable consistency*

Metal or plastic bowl
*About 12 in. in diameter
at the rim, 4 in. in total
height and 6¾ in. in
diameter at the base*

Plywood workboard
*About 3 ft. square,
set on a level area*

Bowl
*Placed upside down
on the plywood*

Cut-away view of the Japanese suiseki stone

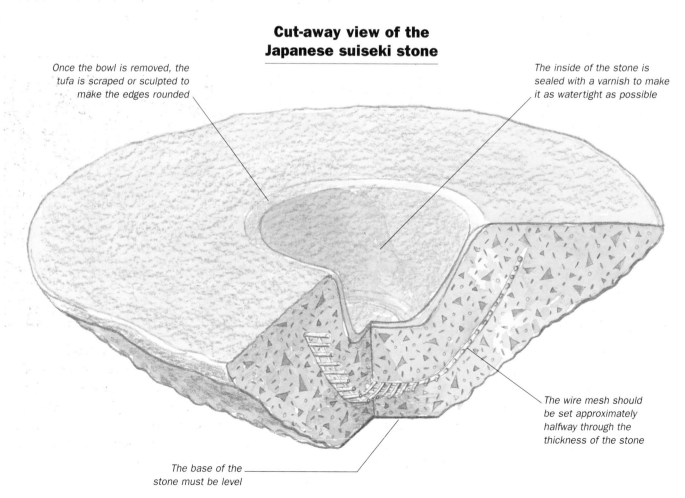

*Once the bowl is removed, the
tufa is scraped or sculpted to
make the edges rounded*

*The inside of the stone is
sealed with a varnish to make
it as watertight as possible*

*The wire mesh should
be set approximately
halfway through the
thickness of the stone*

*The base of the
stone must be level*

Making the Japanese suiseki stone

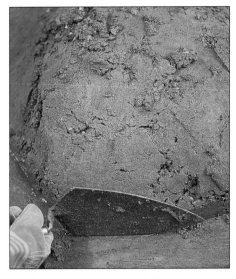

1 Mixing the tufa
Wipe the outside of the bowl with a small amount of water and a lot of soap, until it is slippery. Set it upside down on the workboard. Mix the tufa ingredients with water to form a soft consistency, and start spreading a layer of it over the bowl.

2 Inserting the wire mesh
Build up a layer of hypertufa about 2¾ in. thick, then cut the wire mesh to fit over the mound and press it in. All the edges should be embedded and it must be a tight, close-hugging fit.

3 Completing the mound
Continue adding tufa until the wire mesh is completely covered. Aim for a mound that is irregular in shape and about 32 in. in diameter at the widest part of the rim. Run the trowel around the rim to smooth it.

4 Texturing the surface
Level the top of the mound so that the finished basin will sit flat when it is tipped over. Use your fingers to knead and texture the surface of the sides so that it looks weathered and worn.

5 Painting with varnish
When the tufa is dry, turn the mound over and remove the bowl. Wipe the inside of the depression with mortar. When it has dried, paint a coat of varnish over the mortar to make it waterproof.

6 Setting up the suiseki
Continue to make the surface of the tufa look like weathered stone by scratching and scraping it. Finally, set the suiseki level on your chosen slab of stone, fill it with water, and decorate it with cobblestones and plants.

Old English random paving

If you are intending to build a patio, but do not want to use identical square paving slabs or interlocking pavers, Old English random paving is a good option. It is easy to lay, functional, and the subtle repeat pattern looks good. Although the style is "Old English," the slabs are modern imitation stone made from concrete. This patio is 3 yard square, which allows plenty of space for a table and chairs, or a couple of sun loungers.

Easy

Making time
One weekend
One day for setting out the formwork; one day for laying the concrete and the slabs

Considering the design

The design is based on a grid. The patio is made from three sizes of concrete slabs that look like sandstone: 12 large squares, 18 half-squares, and 16 quarter-squares. However, if you want, the emphasis of the pattern can be changed to a different ratio of small to large squares, or the dimensions of the patio can be changed.

The ground in our site was so firm, dry, and compacted that once the form was in place, we were able to simply fill the frame with concrete and lay the slabs.

However, if the ground in your yard is soft or subject to frost-induced ground heave, then first lay a bed of gravel or crushed stone.

Getting started

Once you have studied your site, draw a grid based on 10 feet square. If you want to vary the ratios of the three different slab sizes from those we have described, to make a different pattern, play around with the various options to work out how many of each type of slab you need.

You will need

Tools

- ✔ Tape measure and straightedge
- ✔ Pegs and string
- ✔ Crosscut saw and claw hammer
- ✔ Spirit level
- ✔ Spade, fork, and shovel
- ✔ Wheelbarrow and bucket
- ✔ Tamping beam: about 5 ft. long, 2⅜ in. wide, and 1⅛ in. thick
- ✔ Club hammer
- ✔ Soft-bristled brush
- ✔ Pointing trowel

Materials

For a patio 10 ft. square

- ✔ Concrete sandstone paving: 12 slabs, 24 in. x 24 in.; 18 slabs, 12 in. x 24 in.; 16 slabs, 12 in. x 12 in.
- ✔ Pine: 5 boards, 10 ft. long, 6 in. wide, and ¾ in. thick (form)
- ✔ Pine: 20 lengths, 12 in. long, 1⅛ in. wide, and ¾ in. thick (form pegs)
- ✔ Old boards to use to walk on
- ✔ Concrete: 1 part (450 lb.) Portland cement, 5 parts (2,250 lb.) aggregate
- ✔ Mortar: 1 part (50 lb.) Portland cement, 3 parts (150 lb.) well-graded mortar sand
- ✔ Nails: 2 lb. of 1½ in.-long nails

Overall dimensions and general notes

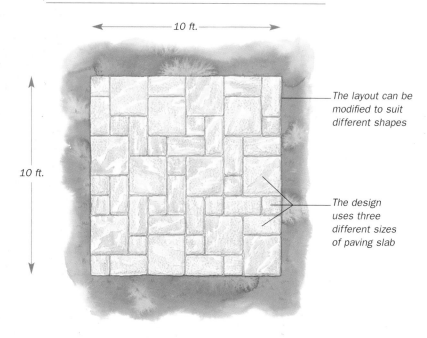

10 ft.

10 ft.

The layout can be modified to suit different shapes

The design uses three different sizes of paving slab

This patio will slot into many styles of garden successfully. The slabs are generally sold in three colors: buff, light sand, and slate gray—choose a single color or a mixture.

Cut-away view of the Old English random paving

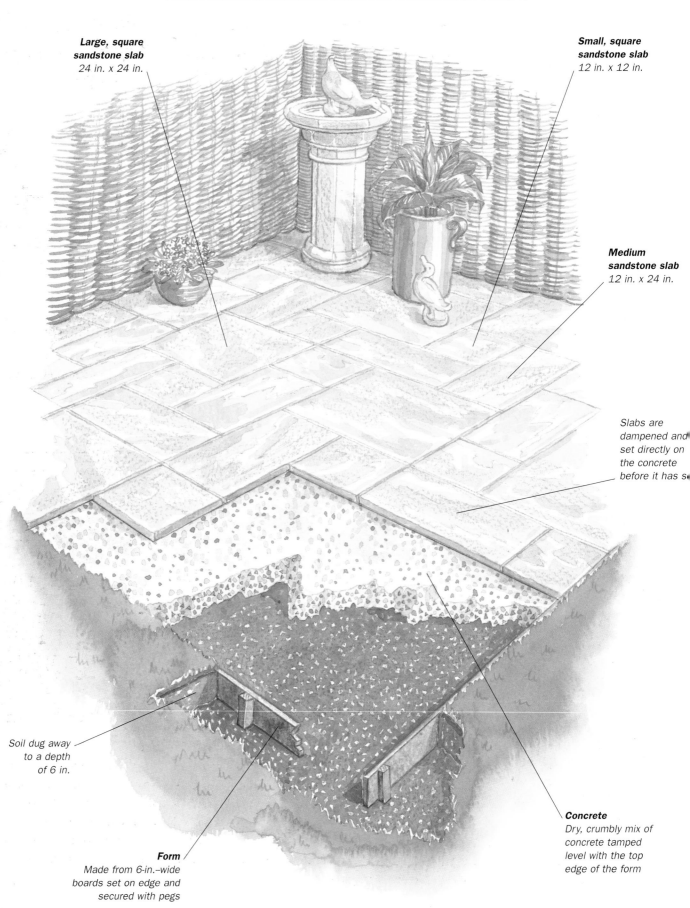

Large, square sandstone slab
24 in. x 24 in.

Small, square sandstone slab
12 in. x 12 in.

Medium sandstone slab
12 in. x 24 in.

Slabs are dampened and set directly on the concrete before it has se

Soil dug away to a depth of 6 in.

Form
Made from 6-in.–wide boards set on edge and secured with pegs

Concrete
Dry, crumbly mix of concrete tamped level with the top edge of the form

Making the Old English random paving

1 Building the form

Measure out the site and set the form boards in place—one on each of the four sides, and one down the middle. Level the boards, then adjust them so that there is a slight slope from one side of the site to another (for drainage, especially away from a building).

2 Laying the concrete

Fix the form boards with form pegs and nails. Make a dry, crumbly mix of concrete, and spread it over the base of the patio. Use the tamping beam to screed, or scrape, the concrete level with the top edge of the form.

3 Laying the slabs

Dampen the back of the slabs, and carefully set them one at a time on the concrete. Use the handle of the club hammer to tap them level to each other.

4 Protecting the slabs

When it is necessary to walk over the slabs, cover them with the old boards so that your weight is evenly spread, which will prevent the slabs from being knocked out of alignment. Step off the boards only when you are laying a slab.

5 Pointing

When the concrete has cured, mix the mortar to a dry, crumbly consistency and use the brush to sweep it between the slabs. Finally, use the pointing trowel to stroke the mortar to a smooth finish. Brush off any excess mortar.

Serpentine walkway

The serpentine walkway is a wonderful solution when you want an exciting and dynamic walkway to wind its way around various features in the garden. Its design also gives you the opportunity to keep your options about the precise shape and route of the walkway open until the last minute. It has been made from gray slabs throughout, but you can use a different color, or even a combination of colors, if desired.

★ ★
Intermediate

Making time
One weekend
One day for preparation, and one day for laying the slabs and finishing details

Overall dimensions and general notes

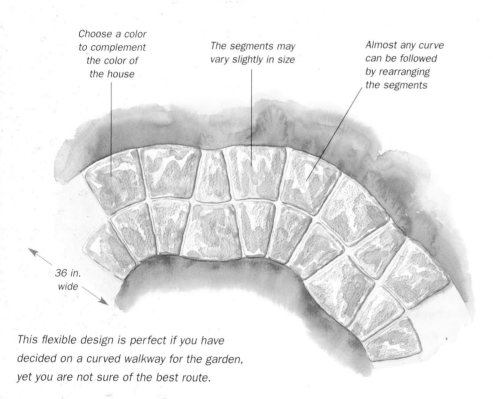

Choose a color to complement the color of the house

The segments may vary slightly in size

Almost any curve can be followed by rearranging the segments

36 in. wide

This flexible design is perfect if you have decided on a curved walkway for the garden, yet you are not sure of the best route.

You will need

Tools

- ✔ Tape measure and chalk
- ✔ Spade, fork, and shovel
- ✔ Wheelbarrow and bucket
- ✔ Rake and stiff-bristled broom
- ✔ Sledgehammer
- ✔ Brick trowel
- ✔ Tamping beam: about 5 ft. long, 2⅜ in. wide, and 1⅛ in. thick
- ✔ Club hammer

Materials

For 12 ft. of walkway, 36 in. wide

- ✔ Middle segment paving slabs (concrete pavers): 12 slabs, 18 in. radius
- ✔ Outer segment paving slabs (concrete pavers): 12 slabs, 18 in. radius
- ✔ Clean sand: about 880 lb.
- ✔ Fine gravel: about 660 lb.
- ✔ Mortar: 1 part (50 lb.) Portland cement, 2 parts (100 lb.) well-graded mortar sand

Considering the design

The walkway is made from the middle and outer slabs in a circular patio kit. The slabs are set in pairs to form two-slab wedges, and alternate wedges are reversed along the course of the walkway.

If you want the walkway to follow a direct route, reverse every other pair of slabs; however, if you want it to bend to run around corners, group the pairs in part-circle curves. The shapes of the slabs allow the walkway to run around bends and over bumps. Using a combination of middle segment and outer segment paving slabs, both measuring 18 inches on the radius line, the walkway works out to be about 36 inches wide. Quantities have been given per 12 feet of walkway—adjust to suit your requirements.

Getting started

Take three or four paired slabs and put them on the lawn. Experiment with various arrangements in order to see how to steer the walkway around gentle and deep curves along the proposed route.

Cut-away view of the serpentine walkway

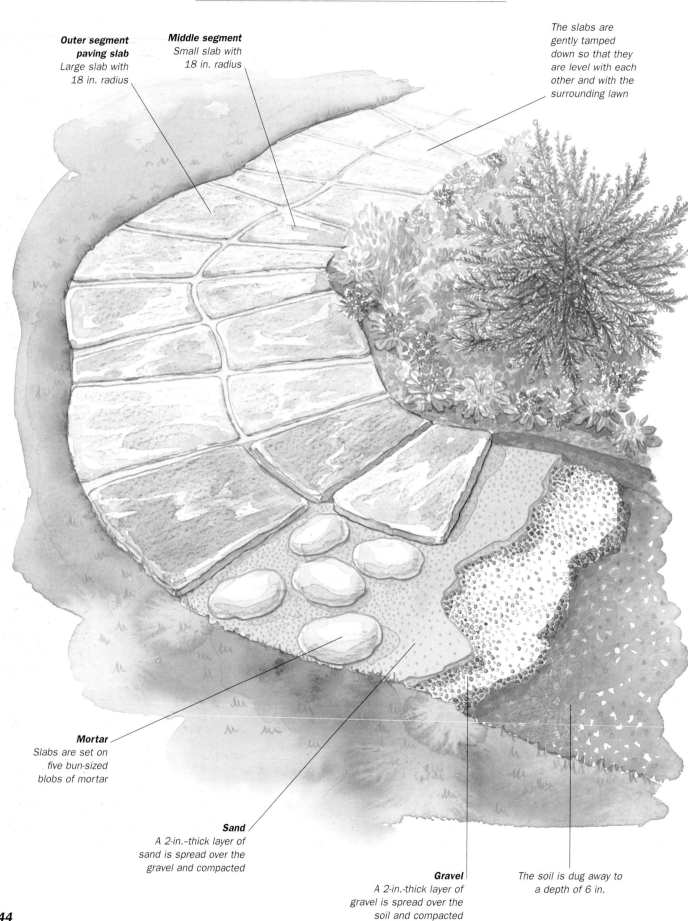

Outer segment paving slab
Large slab with 18 in. radius

Middle segment
Small slab with 18 in. radius

The slabs are gently tamped down so that they are level with each other and with the surrounding lawn

Mortar
Slabs are set on five bun-sized blobs of mortar

Sand
A 2-in.-thick layer of sand is spread over the gravel and compacted

Gravel
A 2-in.-thick layer of gravel is spread over the soil and compacted

The soil is dug away to a depth of 6 in.

Making the serpentine walkway

1 Setting out the slabs
Set the paired middle and outer segment slabs in place on the ground. Make a swift sketch so that you know how they relate to each other. Number the slabs with chalk if desired. Slice around the arrangement with the spade, then move the slabs to one side.

2 Clearing the site
Dig up the turf—you (or a neighbor) may be able to use it elsewhere. Dig out the topsoil (to a depth of about 6 in.) by slicing it into manageable squares, then use the spade, fork, and wheelbarrow to remove it from the site.

3 Making the foundation
Spread and rake a 2-in. layer of gravel over the soil and use the sledgehammer to tamp it down firmly. Shovel sand over the gravel and spread it out until it forms a layer 2 in. thick.

4 Laying the slabs
Dampen the slabs. Set each slab on five generous blobs of mortar, then use the tamping beam and club hammer to tap them level with each other and with the lawn bordering the walkway.

5 Pointing
When the mortar has set (in about two or three hours), sweep the rest of the sand into the joints and around the slabs. Repeat this procedure over several days until the joints feel firm.

Earth-and-stone retaining wall

The technique of building earth-and-stone walls has evolved over many thousands of years. There are no concrete foundations or complex planning involved, just a slow and methodical procedure of studying the shapes of the fieldstones, then fitting them together. If you are planning to build a low raised flowerbed in your garden, and you have a good source of stone, this project provides an absorbing way of constructing it.

Making time
One weekend per 4 yd. of wall
Half a day for the trench; rest of the time for building the wall

Considering the design

The wall is three courses high, plus a course of coping stones to finish the top, and is built entirely from salvaged stone. We used large blocks of rough-cut stone for the primary thick course, thin slices of roof slate to fill in the courses, and square blocks of stone for the coping. The most economical way of building the wall is to use whatever stones are available and modify your technique accordingly.

Earth-and-stone walling is straightforward, but it involves a lot of concentration and coordination between hand and eye. First, a trench is dug and filled with gravel or crushed stone, which is compacted to supply a footing. The first course is laid, consisting of primary stones filled and leveled with secondary stones. Soil is raked down behind the wall, then the second course is laid.

During construction, you will need to check the horizontal level by eye and make sure that the courses are tilted so that, to a small extent, the wall leans back against the bank of soil. Every half yard or so along the courses, the wall must be stabilized by running extra-long stones back into the soil.

Getting started

Work out how long you want your wall to be, divide it by 12 feet, and multiply the stated quantities accordingly. Order the stone. Ideally, you need stone that shows one straight edge and two smooth faces.

You will need

Tools

- ✔ Tape measure and straightedge
- ✔ Pegs and string
- ✔ Spade, fork, and shovel
- ✔ Wheelbarrow and bucket
- ✔ Sledgehammer and club hammer
- ✔ Brick trowel
- ✔ Bricklayer's hammer
- ✔ Brick chisel
- ✔ Old carpet: 12 in. x 24 in.

Materials

For 12 ft. of wall, 22 in. high

- ✔ Salvaged rough-cut stone: ½ cu. yd. (wall and coping)
- ✔ Salvaged roof slate: 1 wheelbarrow load
- ✔ Gravel or crushed stone: 12 bucketfuls

Overall dimensions and general notes

12 ft. long

22 in. high

This is an ideal project when you want to create a retaining wall for a raised flowerbed. You can adjust the length and height of the wall to suit your needs.

Cut-away view of the earth-and-stone retaining wall

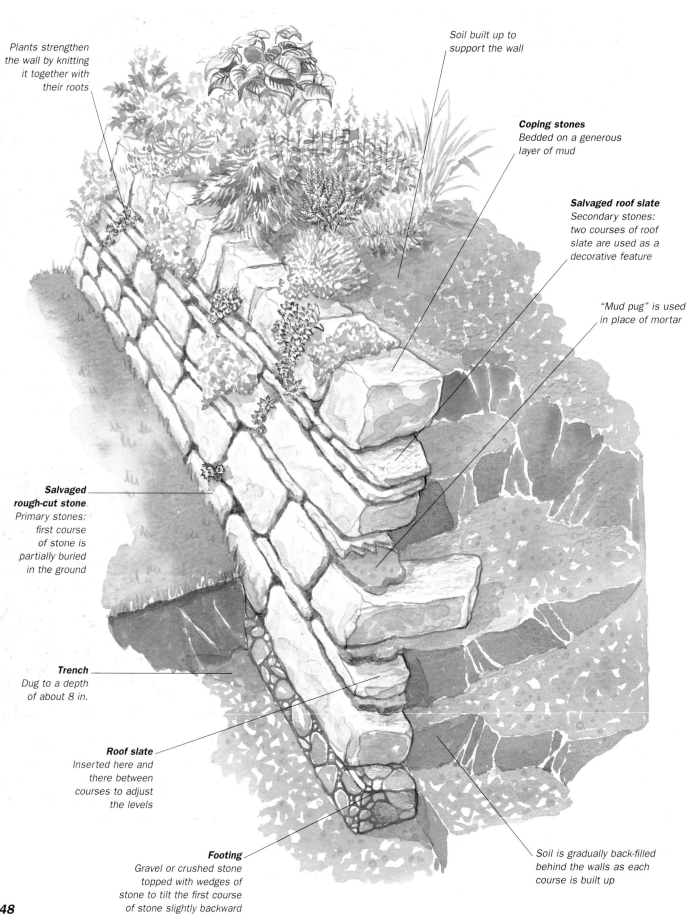

Plants strengthen the wall by knitting it together with their roots

Soil built up to support the wall

Coping stones
Bedded on a generous layer of mud

Salvaged roof slate
Secondary stones: two courses of roof slate are used as a decorative feature

"Mud pug" is used in place of mortar

Salvaged rough-cut stone
Primary stones: first course of stone is partially buried in the ground

Trench
Dug to a depth of about 8 in.

Roof slate
Inserted here and there between courses to adjust the levels

Footing
Gravel or crushed stone topped with wedges of stone to tilt the first course of stone slightly backward

Soil is gradually back-filled behind the walls as each course is built up

Making the earth-and-stone retaining wall

1 Digging a foundation
Dig away the soil down to ground level to reveal the bank of soil that needs retaining. Excavate a trench 12 in. wide and 8 in. deep, and half-fill it with compacted gravel.

2 Making "mud pug"
Take a bucket or so of topsoil and mix it with water until it has the consistency of mortar—this mixture, sometimes known as "mud pug," is used in place of mortar. Remove all the large stones.

3 Laying the first course
Lay the first course of stones on the leveled gravel, with wedges or slivers of roof slate underneath to ensure that the course is angled slightly backward. Rake soil down from the bank to back-fill behind the course. Compact the soil with the club hammer.

4 Leveling the course of stone
Use roof slate to bring all the stones of the first course up to the same level. Trowel a generous layer of mud over the top of the course and lay the roof slate (trim with the bricklayer's hammer as necessary). Run long stones into the bank to provide extra support.

5 Building further courses
If necessary, use the club hammer and brick chisel to cut and trim stone, resting it on the old piece of carpet. Trowel mud into any cavities, and tap misfitting stones back into line. Adjust individual stones by banging small slivers of waste stone into the mud.

6 Bedding the coping stones
Continue building the wall until it is three courses high. Now trowel a layer of mud over the top course, and bed the coping stones in place.

Japanese rock garden

★ ★
Intermediate

Traditional Japanese gardens often incorporate a bridge in their design, to symbolize our journey through life. This Japanese-inspired rock garden includes a stepping-stone bridge and other symbolic features, such as a lantern to represent a guiding light, and shards of weathered crushed stone to depict water. If you want to create an original rock garden with a philosophical twist, this project will provide a great talking point.

Making time
One weekend
One day for selecting the stones, and one day for building the rock garden

Overall dimensions and general notes

← 15 ft. long →

6 ft. wide

This rock garden is simply an arrangement of beautiful stones with a hand-built lantern as the central feature, and it is suited to any modern garden. The size of the rock garden can be adjusted to suit a smaller space. If you prefer, you could use a shop-bought lantern.

You will need

Tools

✔ Tape measure, knife, straightedge

✔ Pegs and string

✔ Spade, fork, shovel, wheelbarrow, bucket, pointing trowel, spirit level

Materials

For a rock garden 15 ft. long and 6 ft. wide

✔ Block of salvaged, weathered, cut stone: 16 in. long and 6 in. square (lantern column)

✔ Slab of salvaged, weathered, cut stone: 8 in. square and 2–2⅜ in. thick (lantern table)

✔ Sandstone: 20 pieces, about 2 in. in diameter (lantern pillars)

✔ Slab of salvaged, weathered, cut stone: 6 in. square and 2–2⅜ in. thick (lantern roof)

✔ Large feature stone: about 3 in. in diameter (finial cobblestone)

✔ Split sandstone: 7 or 8 large slices, about 12–16 in. wide (stepping stones)

✔ Boulders: about 6, ranging in size from 6–16 in. in diameter, in colors and textures to suit ("mountains")

✔ Crushed stone, weathered slate: 100 lb., plum color ("water")

✔ Gravel: 330 lb. ("shore")

✔ Woven plastic sheet: 6 ft. x 15 ft.

✔ Mortar: 1 part (5 lb.) Portland cement, 1 part (5 lb.) lime, 4 parts (10 lb.) well-graded mortar sand

Considering the design

The rock garden measures about 15 feet long and 6 feet wide. It has crushed stone to suggest a turbulent flow of water, fine gravel to mark the shore at the water's edge, large sandstone slabs to form a bridge over the water, rocks that resemble mountains and symbolize barriers, and a stone lantern that indicates light, hope, and guidance.

You can choose just about any stones you desire for the stepping stones and the "water", but the lantern requires rocks of a certain shape and size. The main column is 16 inches long and 6 inches square, with 4 inches of its length buried in the ground. The table at the top of the column is 8 inches square, and the lantern roof is 6 inches square.

Getting started

Take a pencil, tape measure, and a notepad to the stone yard, and study what is available. Select stones and rocks for the various components and lay them on the ground to see how they look together.

Exploded view of the Japanese rock garden

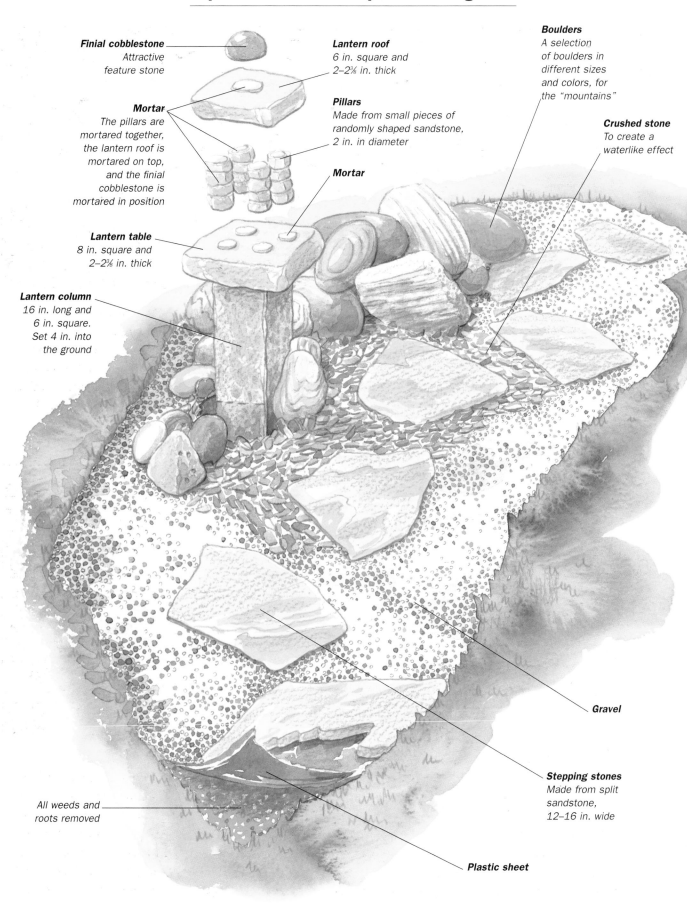

Finial cobblestone
*Attractive
feature stone*

Mortar
*The pillars are
mortared together,
the lantern roof is
mortared on top,
and the finial
cobblestone is
mortared in position*

Lantern table
*8 in. square and
2–2⅜ in. thick*

Lantern column
*16 in. long and
6 in. square.
Set 4 in. into
the ground*

Lantern roof
*6 in. square and
2–2⅜ in. thick*

Pillars
*Made from small pieces of
randomly shaped sandstone,
2 in. in diameter*

Mortar

Boulders
*A selection
of boulders in
different sizes
and colors, for
the "mountains"*

Crushed stone
*To create a
waterlike effect*

Gravel

Stepping stones
*Made from split
sandstone,
12–16 in. wide*

*All weeds and
roots removed*

Plastic sheet

Making the Japanese rock garden

1 Digging the column hole
Measure out the site and stand the lantern column in the most suitable position. Mark around it with the spade, move the stone, and dig a hole to a depth of about 4 in.

2 Laying the plastic
Spread the plastic sheet over the site and cut a hole in it, aligned with the hole in the ground. Lower the lantern column into the hole and check that it is upright. Fold under the outer edges of the sheet to match the shape of the site.

3 Placing the stones
Start to arrange the rock garden stones—the stepping stones for the bridge over the water and the boulders to act as the mountain range. Consider your use of shape and color carefully.

4 Arranging the crushed stone
Spread the plum-colored crushed stone in and around the stones to suggest flow of water. Add gravel along its borders to create a shore. Take your time, standing back often to study the arrangement. Follow your own design instincts.

5 Finishing
Spread mortar on top of the lantern column and set the table stones in place. Mortar the little sandstones upon each other to make pillars. Mortar the roof slate and the finial cobblestone. Spread the rest of the gravel over the plastic sheet, making sure it is fully covered.

Stone and brick walkway

★ ★
Intermediate

Making time
One weekend
One day for putting down the sand, and one day for laying the stones and bricks

The stone (we used concrete pavers) and brick walkway is ideal—it makes an excellent walkway, the surface is sturdy enough for a wheelbarrow to be pushed along it, and it is perfect when you want to build a walkway across a lawn. The flexibility of the flow of bricks neatly does away with the need for a lot of forward planning. Best of all, you can mow straight over the whole walkway without damaging your lawnmower.

Considering the design

Because of the firm and stony nature of the topsoil in our garden, we laid the walkway with only a thick layer of sand as a foundation. However, if your soil is soft and boggy or you live in a frost-induced ground-heave area, lay down a layer of gravel or crushed stone prior to the sand.

Getting started

The quantities we have given are for a walkway that is 3 feet wide and 10 feet long. Study your lawn and consider the route for the walkway. Measure the length of walkway required, then modify the quantities accordingly. Decide what you are going to do with the excavated turf and topsoil.

Start with a dry run to check the placement of the concrete pavers and bricks. Then remove the turf, compact the soil, and put down the sand foundation. Position the bricks, add extra sand where the pavers will go to make up the difference in thickness between bricks and pavers, and lay the pavers. Push soil into the spaces between the bricks and the pavers, and sprinkle with grass seed.

You will need

Tools

- ✔ Tape measure and straightedge
- ✔ Spade, fork ,and shovel
- ✔ Wheelbarrow and bucket
- ✔ Rake
- ✔ Sledgehammer
- ✔ Brick trowel
- ✔ Club hammer
- ✔ Tamping beam: about 5 ft. long, 2⅜ in. wide, and 1⅛ in. thick
- ✔ Stiff-bristled broom

Materials

For a path 10 ft. long and 3 ft. wide

- ✔ Concrete pavers: 112 components 3⅜–4 in. square and 2 in. thick, charcoal color
- ✔ Bricks: 32 bricks, 9 in. long, 4½ in. wide, and 3 in. thick, color and texture to suit
- ✔ Sand: about 300 lb.
- ✔ Topsoil: about 150 lb.
- ✔ Grass seed: about 9 good handfuls
- ✔ Wooden workboards to protect the lawn: size and number will depend on your situation

Overall dimensions and general notes

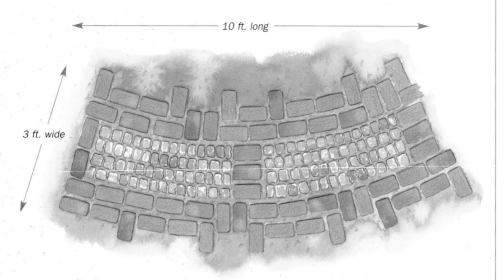

10 ft. long

3 ft. wide

This traditional walkway built from a mixture of bricks and pavers (you can use natural stone instead) looks especially good in an "Old World" setting. It is easy to build and does not use cement, so take as much time as you want to lay the bricks and stones.

Cut-away view of the stone and brick walkway

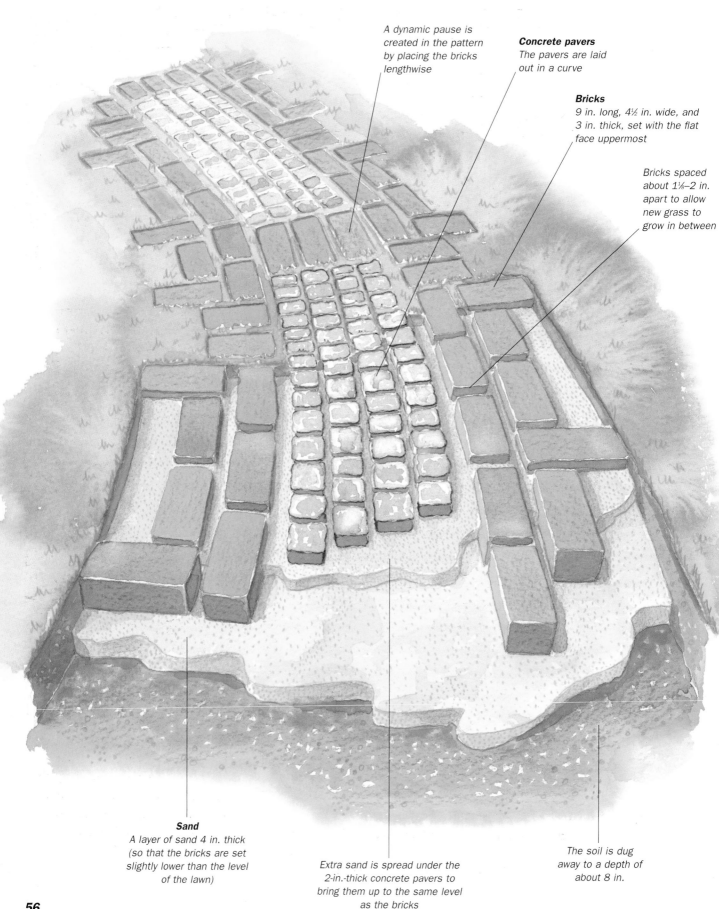

A dynamic pause is created in the pattern by placing the bricks lengthwise

Concrete pavers
The pavers are laid out in a curve

Bricks
9 in. long, 4½ in. wide, and 3 in. thick, set with the flat face uppermost

Bricks spaced about 1⅛–2 in. apart to allow new grass to grow in between

Sand
A layer of sand 4 in. thick (so that the bricks are set slightly lower than the level of the lawn)

Extra sand is spread under the 2-in.-thick concrete pavers to bring them up to the same level as the bricks

The soil is dug away to a depth of about 8 in.

Making the stone and brick walkway

1 Checking the placement
Position the pavers on the lawn and arrange the bricks so that there is uniform spacing of about 1⅛–2 in. between the various components. Make a swift sketch so that you know what goes where.

2 Removing the turf
Slice around the arrangement with the spade. Remove the pavers and bricks, and cut the turf into manageable squares. Use the fork and wheelbarrow to remove the turf from the site.

3 Laying the sand
Rake the soil level and compact it with the sledgehammer. Spread a 4-in.-thick layer of sand over the soil and rake it so that it looks more or less level with the surrounding lawn.

4 Positioning the pavers
Place the pavers into position down the middle of the walkway. Place the bricks on either side of the pavers, using uniform spacing of 1⅛-2 in. With club hammer and beam, tamp them level with each other and a bit lower than the lawn.

5 Finishing
Lay the pavers on an extra layer of sand to bring them up level with the bricks and the lawn. Brush the topsoil into the joints, tamp everything level, and sprinkle grass seed in the joints.

Plinth and slab table

★ ★
Intermediate

Making time
One weekend
*One day for casting
the foundation slab,
and one day for
building the table*

This table is a simple idea—just a single slab of stone set on a low plinth, and it is

reminiscent of Eastern garden designs. Use it for drinks or for serving afternoon

snacks. The beauty of this piece of furniture is that it is weatherproof and doesn't

need to be taken in at the end of the day. It can also double as a display plinth,

ideal for showing containers of plants or a favorite piece of sculpture.

Considering the design

The table is straightforward—it consists of three courses of split sandstone topped with a large flagstone, all mounted on a concrete foundation slab. The plinth stands about 12 inches high, and the tabletop is 24 inches x 26 inches.

Visit a stone yard to obtain materials—the best way to make your choice is to chalk out the 16 inch x 18 inch plan view on the ground, and carefully select enough pieces of 4-inch-thick stone to complete the three courses. Allow one or two extra stones for each course (so you can choose the best fit when you get home) and include 12 good, square-cut corner stones—4 for each course. Choose a single flagstone for the tabletop, which shows one good face.

Getting started

Select the site and stack the stones so that they are nearby. Build the form, making the interior dimensions 16 inches long and 18 inches wide. Set it in position in your garden. Cut around the frame and remove the turf and soil to a depth of 4 inches. Level the frame in the recess.

You will need

Tools

- ✔ Tape measure, chalk, spirit level
- ✔ Crosscut saw and claw hammer
- ✔ Spade and shovel
- ✔ Tamping beam: 24 in. long, 3⅛ in. wide, and 2 in. thick
- ✔ Workboards: planks and pieces of hardboard to protect the area around the site
- ✔ Club hammer and brick chisel
- ✔ Bricklayer's hammer
- ✔ Brick and pointing trowels

Materials

For a table 26 in. long, 24 in. wide, and 15 in. high

- ✔ Flagstone: 1 salvaged slate/sandstone/limestone flagstone, 26 in. long, 24 in. wide, and 2¾ in. thick
- ✔ Split sandstone: 1 sq. yd. of sandstone (pieces about 4¾–9¾ in. long, 2–6 in. wide, and 4 in. thick)
- ✔ Concrete: 1 part (20 lb.) Portland cement, 2 parts (40 lb.) sand, 3 parts (60 lb.) aggregate
- ✔ Mortar: 2 parts (52 lb.) Portland cement, 1 part (26 lb.) lime, 9 parts (234 lb.) well-graded mortar sand
- ✔ Pine: 1 piece rough-sawn pine, 6 ft. long, 3⅛ in. wide, and 2 in. thick (form)
- ✔ Nails: 4 x 4-in.-long nails

Overall dimensions and general notes

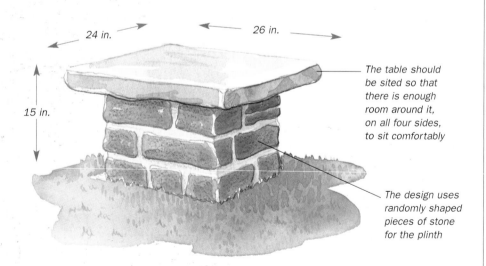

24 in.

26 in.

15 in.

The table should be sited so that there is enough room around it, on all four sides, to sit comfortably

The design uses randomly shaped pieces of stone for the plinth

This timeless design will suit almost any style and size of garden and will last a lifetime. It is constructed from natural stone instead of the concrete paver variety, so it requires a little bit of patience to select and arrange the parts into a pleasing whole.

Exploded view of the plinth and slab table

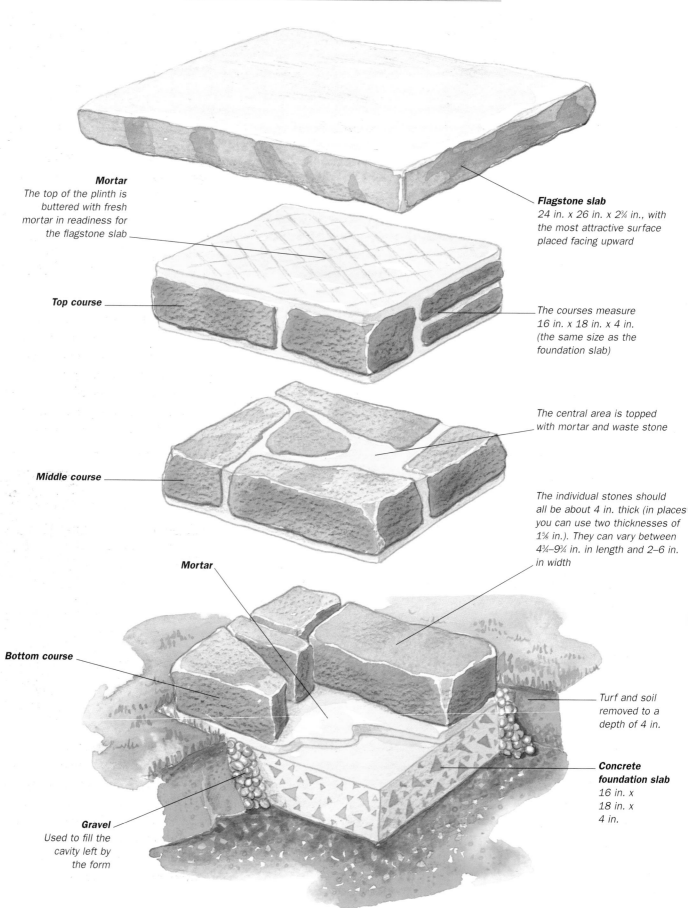

Mortar
The top of the plinth is buttered with fresh mortar in readiness for the flagstone slab

Flagstone slab
24 in. x 26 in. x 2¾ in., with the most attractive surface placed facing upward

Top course

The courses measure 16 in. x 18 in. x 4 in. (the same size as the foundation slab)

Middle course

The central area is topped with mortar and waste stone

The individual stones should all be about 4 in. thick (in places you can use two thicknesses of 1⅞ in.). They can vary between 4¾–9¾ in. in length and 2–6 in. in width

Mortar

Bottom course

Turf and soil removed to a depth of 4 in.

Concrete foundation slab
16 in. x 18 in. x 4 in.

Gravel
Used to fill the cavity left by the form

Making the plinth and slab table

1 Making the frame
Set the wooden form frame in the excavation, wedge it level with stones, and check with the spirit level. (Fill the frame with concrete. Use the tamping beam to level the concrete with the top edge of the frame. Allow to set. The form is removed later.)

2 Trial layout
Protect the area around the concrete foundation with workboards. Arrange the pieces of stone on the foundation so that you have all the makings for three 4-in.-high courses. From course to course, make sure the vertical joints are staggered.

3 Breaking stone
To break a piece of stone, set the stone on the grass, position the brick chisel firmly on the line of cut, and give it one or more well-placed blows with the club hammer. Make sure that you wear goggles and gloves. Use the bricklayer's hammer to trim stone.

4 Laying the first course
Spread a generous layer of mortar over the foundation and lay the first course of stones. Use the weight of the club hammer to gently tap the stones level. Check with the spirit level.

5 Second and third courses
Repeat the procedure to build the other two courses. Fill the central area of the plinth with a mixture of mortar and fragments of waste stone. Use the pointing trowel to tidy up the mortar in the joints of the courses.

6 Laying the flagstone
When you have achieved a level, square pillar, spread a generous layer of fresh mortar over the top of the stack. Dampen the underside of the flagstone slab and get help to gently lower it into position. Pour gravel into the slot between the plinth and the grass.

Boulder and coping wall

This little wall is charming in its simplicity and directness. You don't have to engage in a lot of forward planning—simply order a heap of random split sandstone and a limestone boulder for every yard of wall, then start building. The more challenging part is building the scalloped coping, but it is a lot fun to do. An added advantage is that the modest weight of the components means that the project is open to everyone.

★★
Intermediate

Making time
One weekend for every 10 ft. of wa

One day for building the basic wall, and or day for the coping

Overall dimensions and general notes

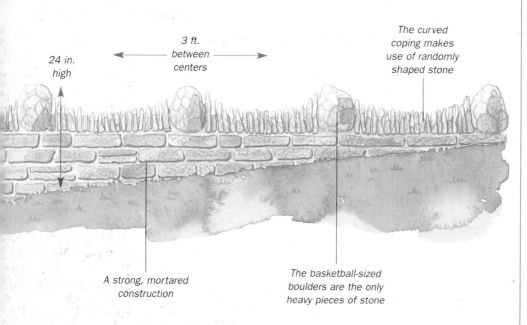

24 in. high

3 ft. between centers

The curved coping makes use of randomly shaped stone

A strong, mortared construction

The basketball-sized boulders are the only heavy pieces of stone

The project produces a low, decorative wall. It is perfect for creating a raised flowerbed— simply build end walls, fill with a layer of gravel for drainage, top with soil, and plant up.

Considering the design

The wall is built starting just below ground level, with the first course of stone set on a layer of compacted waste stone. First, dig a shallow trench, tamp all the pieces of waste stone into the bottom of it with a sledgehammer, then set the first course in the trench so that it is just below ground level.

When the wall is about three or four courses high, the top of the wall is buttered with a generous wedge of mortar, and the boulder and stone slices for the coping are set in place. All you do is mark in the position of the boulders, and the halfway point between them. Then set the first boulder in place and arrange the coping so that the pieces descend in size up to the midway point, then increase in size up to the next boulder.

Getting started

Work out how long you want your wall to be. The quantities given are per 3 feet of wall: multiply as necessary. Visit the stone yard, discuss what you are planning to build, and choose some attractive boulders and random split sandstone.

You will need

Tools

- ✔ Tape measure
- ✔ Pegs and string
- ✔ Spade, fork, and shovel
- ✔ Wheelbarrow and bucket
- ✔ Sledgehammer
- ✔ Brick trowel
- ✔ Club hammer
- ✔ Bricklayer's hammer
- ✔ Pointing trowel
- ✔ Old hand brush

Materials

For 3 ft. of wall, 24 in. high

- ✔ Sandstone: about 2 wheelbarrow loads of random stones in various sizes and thicknesses
- ✔ Limestone boulder: 1 large, basketball-sized stone
- ✔ Waste stone: 9 bucketfuls
- ✔ Mortar: 1 part (50 lb.) Portland cement, 3 parts (150 lb.) well-graded mortar sand

Cut-away view of the boulder and coping wall

Limestone boulder
These feature stones are set about 32–36 in. apart

Coping stones
Set on edge and bedded in mortar

Stones ranging from large to small, then back to large—to create the characteristic scalloped necklace pattern

Banked soil supports the wall

Trench
Dug out to the depth and width of a spade (about 6¼ in. wide and 9¾ in. deep)

The vertical joints must be staggered

First course of stone bedded on a generous layer of mortar

Trench half-filled with compacted waste stone

Making the boulder and coping wall

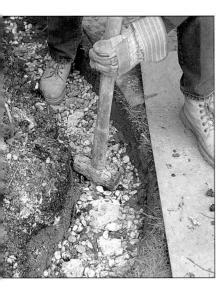

1 Marking out
Use the string and pegs to mark out the dimensions of the wall. Dig a trench the depth and width of a spade (about 6¼ in. wide and 9¾ in. deep). Half-fill the trench with waste stone and compact it with the sledgehammer.

2 Laying the first course
Trowel a generous layer of mortar into the trench and set the first course of stone in place. Check the level by eye and use the club hammer to make adjustments. Rake soil behind the inside face of the wall to support it.

3 Adding more courses
Continue building one course upon another, all the while doing your best to ensure that the vertical joints are staggered. Fill the cavities with mortar and slivers of sandstone.

4 Placing the boulders
Generously butter the top of the wall with mortar. Mark the positions of the boulders and halfway points between them. Place the first boulder, then range slices of stone on edge, running in a scallop pattern to the next boulder. Use the bricklayer's hammer to trim stones.

5 Pointing
Finally, use the pointing trowel to fill the joints with mortar. Sculpt the uppermost wedge of mortar, between the coping stones and the rest of the wall, so that it angles down from the coping. Tidy up the joints and brush off extra mortar.

Inlay block steps

★ ★ ★
Advanced

This is the ideal project for a minimalist. If you have a crisp, modern home with a lot of glass and concrete painted in flat colors, inlay block steps in the yard will complement it perfectly. This simple flight of steps can be built with the minimum of fuss. Each step is decorated with a small amount of detailing, made up of slivers of crushed stone arranged in an attractive basketweave pattern.

Making time
One weekend
One day for getting the flight of steps into place; one day for the detailing and finishing

Considering the design

Each step consists of two hollow concrete blocks, making a 17-inch square. The whole flight is dug into the ground and the top step is flush with ground level. This technique negates the need both for complex measuring and for side retaining walls. Each step stands clear and separate from its neighbor. Once the blocks are in place, the hollows in them are filled with concrete, topped with mortar, and studded with stone, both for decorative effect and to provide a firm footing.

Getting started

Once you have accepted the delivery of the blocks, play around with various arrangements until you have a clear picture of how they relate to each other. Make a sketch and take measurements.

You will need

Tools

- ✔ Tape measure and straightedge
- ✔ Pegs and string
- ✔ Spade, fork, and shovel
- ✔ Spirit levels: one long and one short
- ✔ Wheelbarrow and bucket
- ✔ Brick trowel
- ✔ Pointing trowel
- ✔ Soft-bristled brush
- ✔ Paintbrush

Materials

For a flight of steps about 5 ft. 6 in. long and 17 in. wide

- ✔ Hollow concrete building blocks: 8 blocks, 17 in. long, 8¼ in. wide, and 8¼ in. thick
- ✔ Crushed stone, plum-colored slate: 55 lb.
- ✔ Rocks and cobblestones: 2 wheelbarrow loads (to decorate the site)
- ✔ Concrete: 1 part (44 lb.) Portland cement, 5 parts (220 lb.) aggregate
- ✔ Mortar: 1 part (22 lb.) Portland cement, 2 parts (44 lb.) well-graded mortar sand
- ✔ Paint: exterior-grade matte paint in a color of your choice

Overall dimensions and general notes

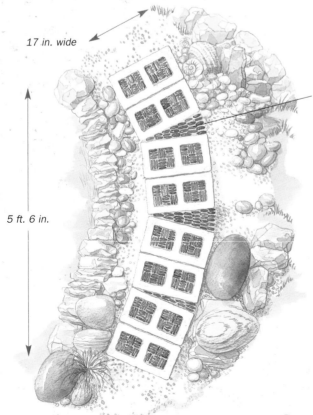

17 in. wide

5 ft. 6 in.

The angles between the steps can be adjusted to suit almost any curve

These steps draw their inspiration from an architect-designed building by the sea. They are particularly easy to build and can be painted in whatever colors you desire.

Exploded view of the inlay block steps

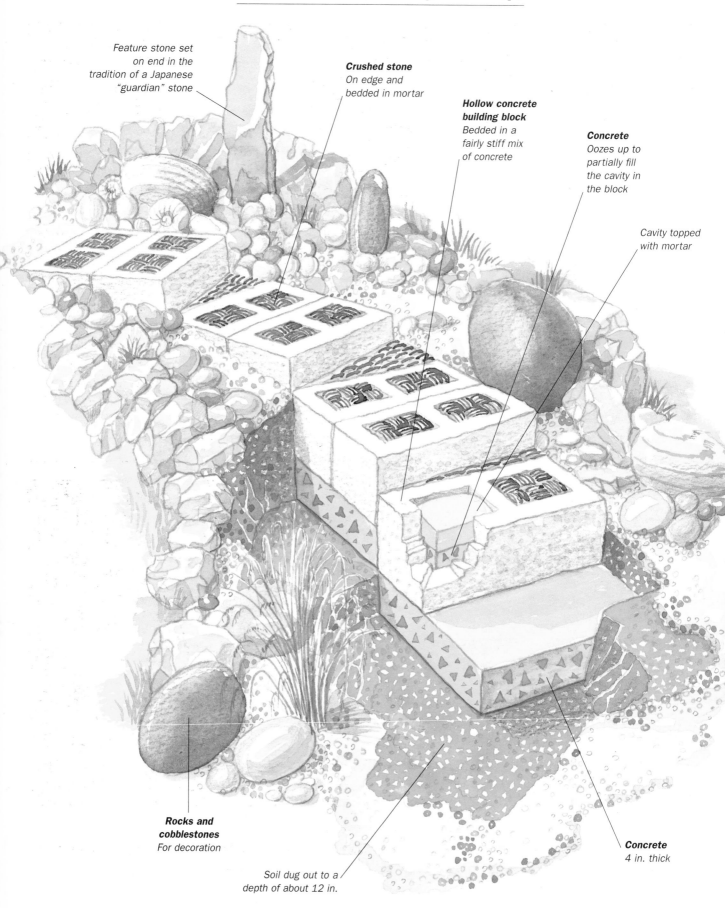

Feature stone set on end in the tradition of a Japanese "guardian" stone

Crushed stone
On edge and bedded in mortar

Hollow concrete building block
Bedded in a fairly stiff mix of concrete

Concrete
Oozes up to partially fill the cavity in the block

Cavity topped with mortar

Rocks and cobblestones
For decoration

Soil dug out to a depth of about 12 in.

Concrete
4 in. thick

Making the inlay block steps

1 Trial arrangement
Arrange the concrete blocks in pairs along the proposed route of the walkway, so that each pair stands separate, and so that the total flight gradually angles to follow the route.

2 Clearing the turf
Use the spade to mark around the pairs of blocks. Remove the blocks, slice away the turf, and dig individual holes to a depth of about 12 in. Use the small spirit level to check that the bottom of the holes are level.

3 Laying the concrete blocks
Make a fairly stiff mix of concrete, spread a 4-in.-thick layer in the bottom of each hole, and set the paired blocks in place. A little concrete will ooze into the cavities. Make adjustments until the blocks are level with each other and with the whole flight.

4 Step inlays
Trowel concrete into the cavities in the blocks, half-filling them, then add mortar to within ³⁄₈ in. of the top. Set the crushed stone in the mortar, forming a basketweave pattern. Check that the surface is flush with the block.

5 Painting and decoration
Brush all dust and debris from the blocks, and paint them in your chosen color. Finally, decorate the site with rocks and cobblestones.

Stone planter

This planter draws its inspiration from the carved stone water troughs seen in fields in northern England. It is made from three courses of concrete pavers made to resemble sandstone, and the top of the planter is finished with a traditional coping technique known as "spotted dick"—no doubt named after the dessert popular in that part of the world. This is a good project for a traditional garden.

Making time
One weekend
One day for laying the foundation slab, and one day for building the walls

Considering the design

Each course is made of nine pavers, one of which has to be cut approximately two-thirds of the way along its length (it is premarked with registration grooves, scored around the paver with a club hammer and brick chisel). Making the coping is plenty of fun. A generous wedge of mortar is spread on top of the finished planter, modeled to a smooth, half-round section, then studded with small pebbles.

Getting started

Decide how long you want your planter to be. Do a trial run with the pavers, so that you will know how the courses will best fit together.

Overall dimensions and general notes

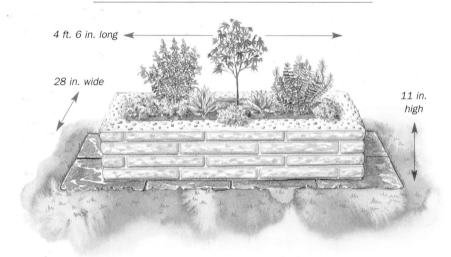

4 ft. 6 in. long

28 in. wide

11 in. high

A stone planter made from concrete pavers is ideal for a small garden. The size of the planter can be adjusted easily, and square or L-shaped configurations are possible.

You will need

Tools

- Tape measure, straightedge, and chalk
- Pegs and string
- Boards to protect the surrounding grass
- Spade, rake, and shovel
- Wheelbarrow and bucket
- Crosscut saw
- Claw hammer
- Spirit level
- Sledgehammer

- Tamping beam: about 1 yd. long, 2⅜ in. wide, and 1⅛ in. thick
- Brick trowel
- Club hammer and brick chisel
- Pointing trowel
- Wire brush and soft-bristled brush

Materials

For a planter 4 ft. 6 in. long, 28 in. wide, and 11 in. high

- Concrete pavers, imitation sandstone: 36 blocks, 17 in. long, 5⅛ in. wide, and 2⅜ in. thick

- Concrete paving slabs: 8 slabs, 18 in. square, color of your choice
- Pebbles: 1 bucketful, size and color of your choice
- Gravel or crushed stone: 2 wheelbarrow loads
- Well-graded mortar sand: 6 wheelbarrow loads
- Mortar: 1 part (66 lb.) Portland cement, 6 parts (396 lb.) well-graded mortar sand
- Pine: 20 ft. long, 3 in. wide, and 1 in. thick (form)
- Nails: 2 lb. of 1½-in.-long nails

Exploded view of the stone planter

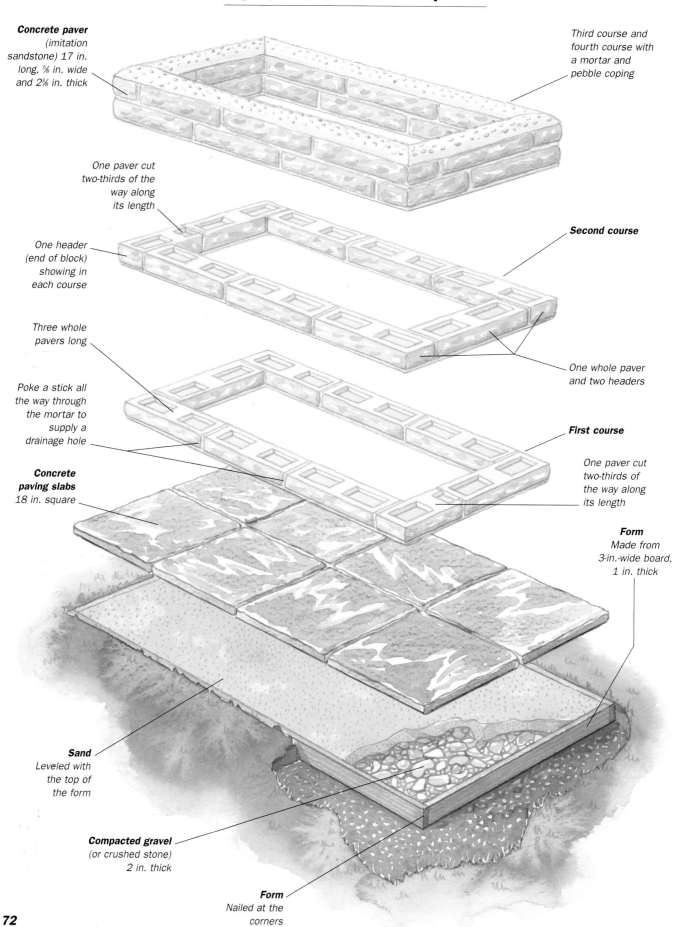

Concrete paver (imitation sandstone) 17 in. long, ⅝ in. wide and 2⅜ in. thick

Third course and fourth course with a mortar and pebble coping

One paver cut two-thirds of the way along its length

One header (end of block) showing in each course

Second course

Three whole pavers long

One whole paver and two headers

Poke a stick all the way through the mortar to supply a drainage hole

First course

Concrete paving slabs 18 in. square

One paver cut two-thirds of the way along its length

Form *Made from 3-in.-wide board, 1 in. thick*

Sand *Leveled with the top of the form*

Compacted gravel (or crushed stone) 2 in. thick

Form *Nailed at the corners*

Cut-away view of the stone planter

Plants
Plant the planter with shrubs, small flowers, herbs, strawberries, or whatever you desire

Planting mixture
To suit your plants

Coping
A half-round mortar coping (shaped by eye using a pointing trowel) is studded with pebbles

Waste stone in the bottom of the planter improves the drainage

Walls
Four courses high (you can build them higher)

The soil is dug out to the depth of a spade (9¾ in. deep)

The form is left in place

Mortar
Each slab is bedded on five blobs of mortar

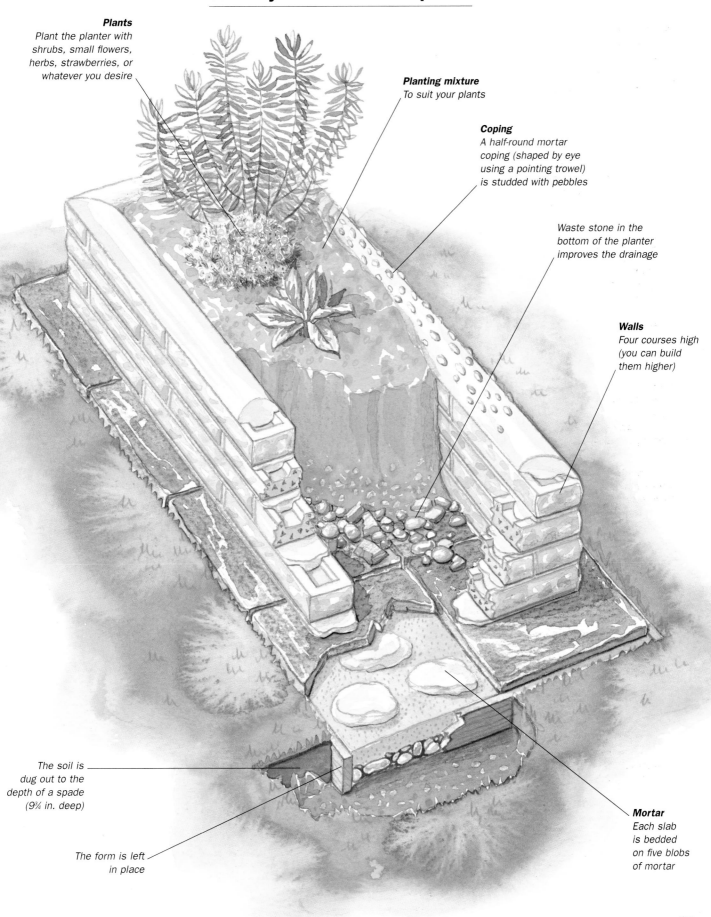

Making the stone planter

1 Form
Measure out the foundation area, making it 3 ft. wide and 6 ft. long. Dig out the area to the depth of the spade. Insert and level the form, and secure it in place with nails. Spread gravel or crushed stone in the form frame, and compact it with the sledgehammer.

2 Spreading the sand
Shovel sand over the gravel bed within the frame and rake it even. Use the tamping beam to compact and level the sand. You should have a firm foundation that is level with the top edge of the form.

3 Making the concrete slab base
Mix the mortar to a smooth, firm consistency. Put five generous, bun-shaped blobs on the sand where the first concrete slab will be positioned. Dampen the back of the slab, and set it carefully in place upon the sand. Repeat with the other slabs.

4 Laying the first course
Use the tape measure, straightedge, and chalk to set out the shape of the planter on the concrete slab base. Have a dry run to place the first course of concrete pavers. Using club hammer and brick chisel, cut one paver to fit. Check that all the pavers fit correctly.

5 Leveling the blocks

Trowel mortar on the concrete slabs, dampen the pavers for the first course, and set them in place. Use the tamping beam, club hammer, and spirit level to ensure that the whole course is level. Insert two drainage holes in the mortar as shown on page 72.

6 Building the other courses

Repeat the procedure to build the other three courses. Make sure that all the joints are full of mortar, but at this stage, do not remove the excess. Keep checking that a course is level before building the next course.

7 Checking with the spirit level

When all four courses are in place, use the tamping beam and spirit level to ensure that the horizontal and vertical levels are true. Tap nonaligned pavers into line with the club hammer.

8 Studding with pebbles

With the pointing trowel, lay a generous coping of mortar on the top course and sculpt it to a smooth, half-rounded finish. Press pebbles into the mortar. Use the trowel, wire brush, and soft-bristled brush to create a good finish on the courses.

Bench with arch detail

This bench is a beautifully dynamic shape, and the building procedure is very satisfying. After you have laid the stone over the form, it is a triumphal moment when you remove the form to see that the arch actually stands unsupported. If you had planned to build a bench in your yard, to sit on or, perhaps, to use as a table, try this project—you will amaze yourself and your friends with your stoneworking skills.

Making time
Two weekends

One day for building the basic arch, and three days for the walls and slabs

Considering the design

The bench is constructed on a base slab (or an existing patio slab). Two pillars are built and plywood sprung between them. Thin slivers of stone are worked into mortar over the plywood, the end and side walls are built up to square off the structure, and, finally, the structure is topped with slabs to create the seat.

Getting started

Start by searching for the stone. You need a small number of square-edged blocks for the two pillars, and a heap of thin, broken sandstone for the arch.

Overall dimensions and general notes

4 ft. long

21 in. high

18 in. wide

This decorative bench has been built on a specially constructed foundation slab, but it can be built directly onto an existing patio. The arch is deceptively easy to make.

You will need

Tools

- ✓ Tape measure, chalk, and straightedge
- ✓ Pegs and string
- ✓ Shovel, wheelbarrow, and bucket
- ✓ Old carpet: about 12 in. x 24 in.
- ✓ Club hammer and brick chisel
- ✓ Bricklayer's hammer
- ✓ Brick trowel
- ✓ Pointing trowel
- ✓ Spirit level
- ✓ Soft-bristled brush

Materials

For a bench 4 ft. long, 18 in. wide, and 21 in. high

- ✓ Sandstone: 1 wheelbarrow load of pieces about 6 in. wide and 2⅜–2¾ in. thick (pillars)
- ✓ Sandstone or salvaged roof slate: 3 wheelbarrow loads of thin split stone (arch and walls)
- ✓ Waste roof slate and broken tiles: 1 bucketful of each (arch)
- ✓ Natural sandstone or concrete pavers: 2 slabs, 18 in. square; 1 slab, 18 in. long and 12 in. wide (seat)
- ✓ Rope-top edging: 12 edging components, 24 in. long, 6 in. high and 2 in. thick, terracotta color (to frame the crushed stone infill)
- ✓ Pillar-and-ball posts: 4 posts, 11 in. high and 2⅜ in. square, terracotta color (to link the edging)
- ✓ Crushed stone, plum-colored slate: 110 lb. (decorative infill)
- ✓ Concrete blocks: 6 blocks, 18 in. long, 8⅝ in. wide, and 4 in. thick (for springing the plywood)
- ✓ Form: a sheet of thin plywood, 3 ft. long, 14 in. wide, and 3/16 in. thick (with the grain running across the width of the plywood)
- ✓ Gravel or crushed stone: 8 wheelbarrow loads
- ✓ Concrete: 1 part (77 lb.) Portland cement, 2 parts (154 lb.) sand, and 3 parts (231 lb.) aggregate
- ✓ Mortar: 1 part (55 lb.) cement and 3 parts (165 lb.) well-graded mortar sand

Exploded view of the bench with arch detail

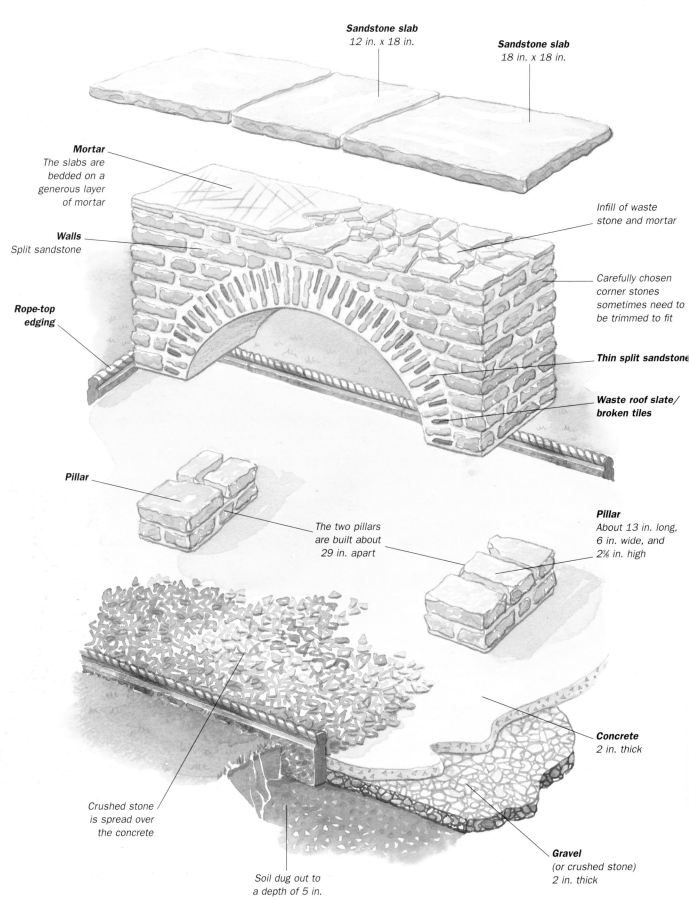

Sandstone slab
12 in. x 18 in.

Sandstone slab
18 in. x 18 in.

Mortar
The slabs are bedded on a generous layer of mortar

Infill of waste stone and mortar

Walls
Split sandstone

Carefully chosen corner stones sometimes need to be trimmed to fit

Rope-top edging

Thin split sandstone

Waste roof slate/ broken tiles

Pillar

The two pillars are built about 29 in. apart

Pillar
About 13 in. long, 6 in. wide, and 2⅜ in. high

Crushed stone is spread over the concrete

Concrete
2 in. thick

Soil dug out to a depth of 5 in.

Gravel
(or crushed stone) 2 in. thick

Detail of the base of the bench

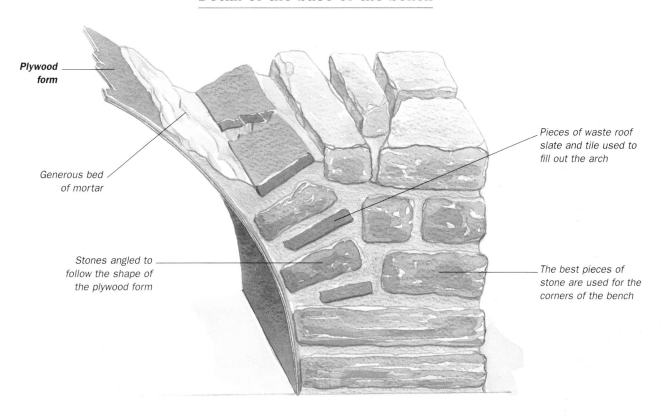

Plywood form

Generous bed of mortar

Stones angled to follow the shape of the plywood form

Pieces of waste roof slate and tile used to fill out the arch

The best pieces of stone are used for the corners of the bench

Cross-section of the bench

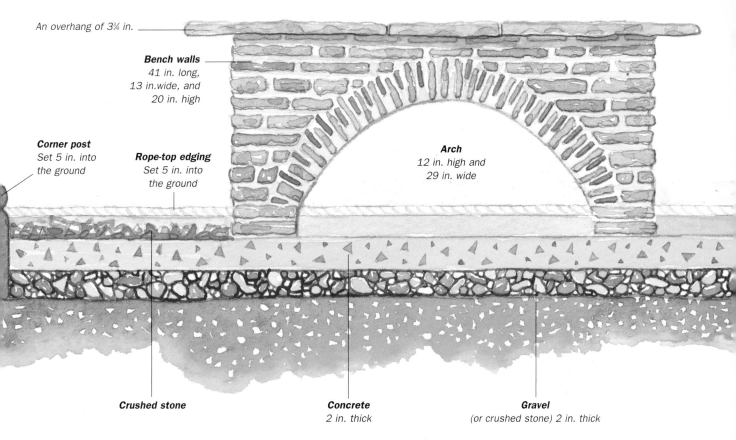

An overhang of 3¾ in.

Bench walls
41 in. long, 13 in. wide, and 20 in. high

Corner post
Set 5 in. into the ground

Rope-top edging
Set 5 in. into the ground

Arch
12 in. high and 29 in. wide

Crushed stone

Concrete
2 in. thick

Gravel
(or crushed stone) 2 in. thick

Making the bench with arch detail

1 Measuring out
Build a concrete base slab if needed. Dig out the soil to a depth of 5 in. and compact 2 in. of gravel or crushed stone in the recess. Lay the concrete. Mark out the seat. The pillars need to measure about 13 in. long, 6 in. wide, and $2^{3}/_{8}$ in. high, and they stand about 29 in. apart.

2 Building the pillars
Build the two pillars in a dry run, making sure that the corners are, as near as possible, at right angles. Cut stone with the club hammer and brick chisel, and trim it with the bricklayer's hammer. Then build the pillars with mortar and allow to set for a few hours.

3 Arch form
Set the concrete blocks around the pillars and spring the sheet of plywood into an arch, so that it is supported by the concrete blocks and is just touching the inside of the pillars.

4 Making the arch
Mix the mortar to a soft, buttery consistency, and lay the thin pieces of slate over the form. Work up from both sides in order to keep the weight equally distributed. Try to keep the sides of the arch aligned with the edge of the plywood.

5 Removing the plywood
When the mortar has set, carefully remove the plywood and the concrete blocks. Lay courses of stone on the pillars, doing your best to ensure that the corners are sharp and square.

6 Checking the structure

Every now and again as you are building the walls, stop and use the spirit level to ensure that the sides of the structure are vertically true. Use a hammer or the handle of the trowel to nudge stones into line.

7 Tidying the mortar

Wait until the mortar is firm (after about two or three hours), then use the end of the pointing trowel to scrape out excess mortar and reveal the edges of the stones to their best advantage, giving the bench a more attractive appearance.

8 Bedding the slabs

Spread a generous layer of mortar over the top of the last course, dampen the back of the seat slabs, and gently bed them in place. Make checks with the spirit level and, if necessary, tamp the slabs level with the handle of the club hammer.

9 Inserting the rope-top edging

Dig a shallow trench around the base slab, and set the rope-top edging and pillar-and-ball posts in place on a bed of mortar. Check the levels with the spirit level. Tidy up the bench with the brush. Finally, fill the area around the bench with crushed stone.

Crazy-paving steps

If you want a low-cost flight of three or four steps, how about making stone crazy-paving steps? The design harks back to the 1920s, and it uses a mixture of natural split sandstone and salvaged cut stone. The low risers make the steps easy to use for everyone, from the very young to older members of the family. The slightly rippled surface of the steps feels good underfoot, and it is also attractive.

Making time
Two weekends
One day for putting in the concrete foundation slab, and three days for building

Considering the design

The steps spring off a single concrete strip foundation slab that runs under the whole flight. The foundation slab is built first, then the first riser, side walls, and back wall. The walls are back-filled with concrete and topped with the crazy paving to make the first tread. Then the next riser wall and related walls are built, back-filled, and so on. We have used random split sandstone for the walls, but you could use limestone, or even a mixture of bricks and stone instead—it depends on your budget and the availability of materials. The height of the riser walls and the depth of the treads are, to a great extent, governed by safety and comfort—low risers are both comfortable and safe to negotiate; however the width of the flight can be shaped to suit the size of your site and your own requirements.

Getting started

Decide how long you want the flight of steps to be. Establish the position and mark out the shape of the foundation slab. Plan how to move around the garden while the steps are being built.

You will need

Tools

- ✔ Tape measure and straightedge
- ✔ Pegs and string
- ✔ Spade, fork, and shovel
- ✔ Sledgehammer
- ✔ Wheelbarrow and bucket
- ✔ Tamping beam: about 5 ft. long, 2⅜ in. wide, and 1⅛ in. thick
- ✔ Club hammer and claw hammer
- ✔ Bricklayer's hammer
- ✔ Brick and pointing trowels
- ✔ Spirit level
- ✔ Soft-bristled brush

Materials

For two steps, each 3 ft. wide, 24 in. deep, and 7¼ in. high

- ✔ Sandstone: about 1.2 sq. yd. split stone in random sizes and thicknesses (amount allows for wastage and choice)
- ✔ Waste stone: about 10 wheelbarrow loads
- ✔ Pine: 26 ft. long, 2⅜ in. wide, and 1⅛ in. thick (form)
- ✔ Concrete: 1 part (220 lb.) Portland cement, 5 parts (1,100 lb.) aggregate
- ✔ Mortar: 1 part (110 lb.) Portland cement, 3 parts (330 lb.) well-graded mortar sand
- ✔ Nails: 12 x 2–in. long nails

Overall dimensions and general notes

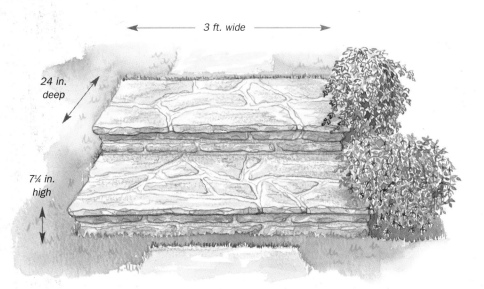

3 ft. wide

24 in. deep

7¼ in. high

A good project for a rural or urban garden, crazy paving is an attractive and practical surface for steps (it provides a lot of grip). The width, height, and depth of the steps can be adjusted to suit your requirements and the slope of the site.

Exploded view of the crazy-paving steps

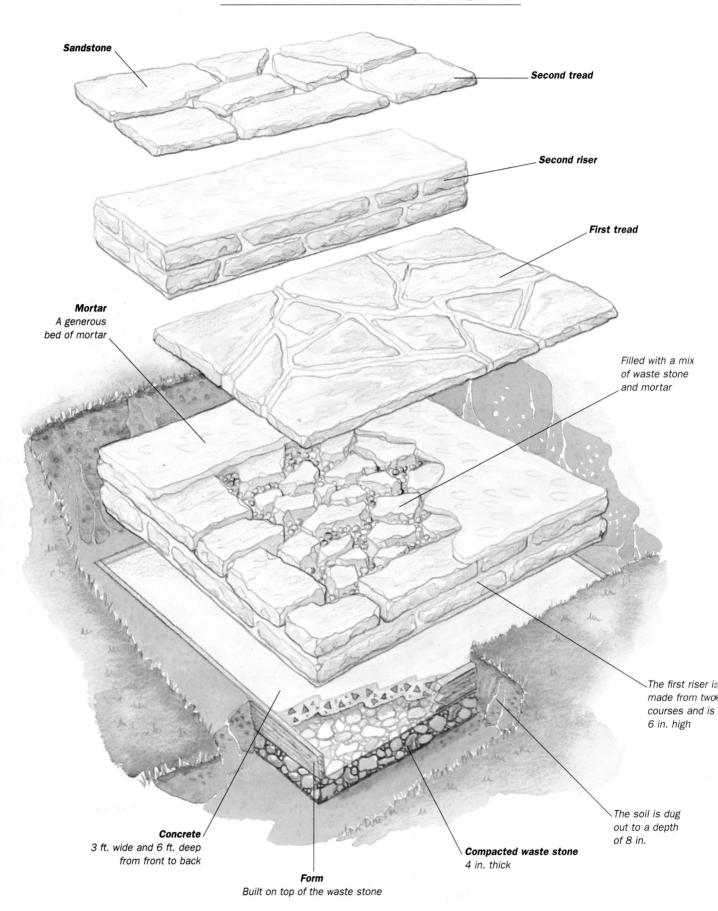

Sandstone

Second tread

Second riser

First tread

Mortar
A generous
bed of mortar

Filled with a mix
of waste stone
and mortar

The first riser is
made from two
courses and is
6 in. high

The soil is dug
out to a depth
of 8 in.

Concrete
3 ft. wide and 6 ft. deep
from front to back

Form
Built on top of the waste stone

Compacted waste stone
4 in. thick

Cut-away view of the crazy-paving steps

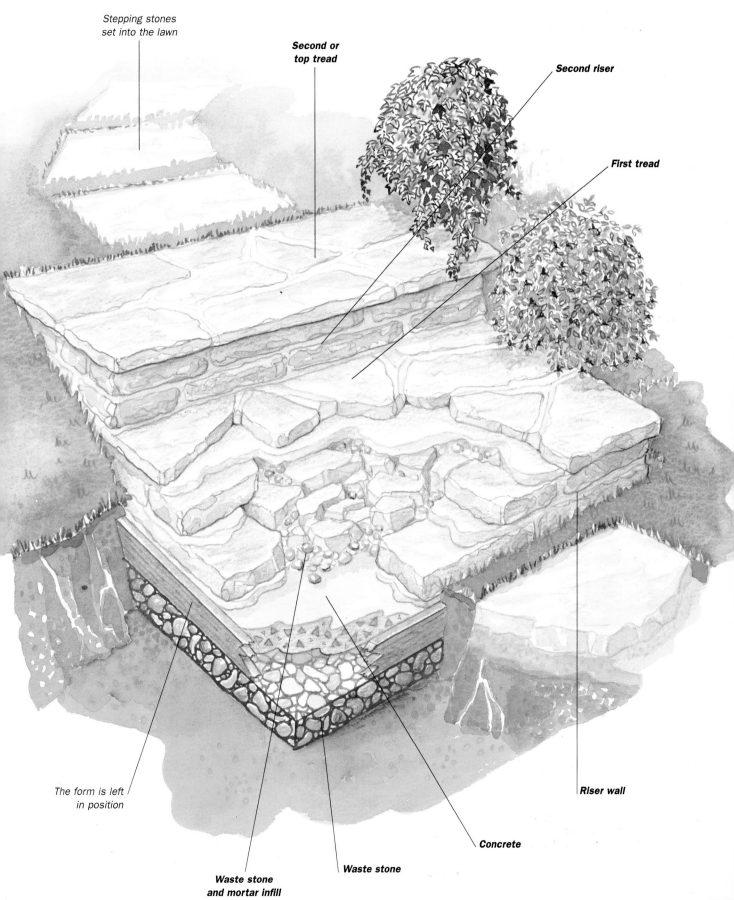

Stepping stones
set into the lawn

Second or
top tread

Second riser

First tread

The form is left
in position

Riser wall

Concrete

Waste stone

Waste stone
and mortar infill

Making the crazy-paving steps

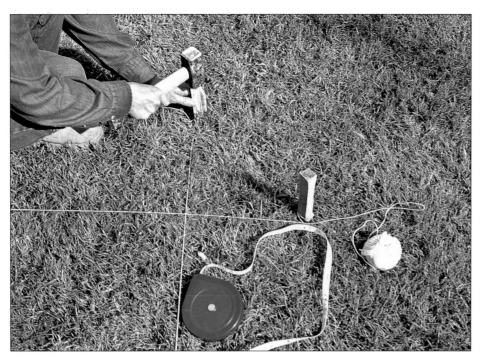

2 Making the foundation slab
Dig out the soil to a depth of 8 in. Half-fill the recess with waste stone and compact it with the sledgehammer. Secure the form and fit it into place. Top the waste stone with a 4-in.-thick layer of concrete, leveling it with the tamping beam.

1 Marking out
Use the tape measure, pegs, and string to mark out the overall size and shape of the foundation slab, which is 3 ft. wide and 6 ft. from front to back. Remove the turf, in squares, from the site (use elsewhere in the garden or give to a friend).

3 Setting out the first step
Use the tape measure, straightedge, and chalk to set out the position of the first riser wall, side walls, and back wall on the concrete slab. Select stones and lay them out dry. The border is 12 in. wide. Make joints as small as possible and use right-angled stones for corners.

4 Building the first step
Mix the mortar to a buttery consistency and build the riser wall, side walls, and back wall to a height of 6 in.. Back-fill the area within the walls with 5 in. of waste stone and leftover mortar. Top the central area with concrete and level off.

5 Bedding the crazy paving
When the concrete has set, select stones for the crazy paving and lay them on top. Trowel mortar on the concrete and bed the crazy paving in place. Arrange the stones so that there is an overhang to the tread of about ¾ in. at the front and side edges.

6 Building the other steps
Measure back 24 in. from the edge of the tread, establishing the depth of the tread and the position of the riser wall for the next step. Repeat the procedure already described to build the next step. Keep checking that everything is level.

8 Pointing
Use the pointing trowel and some freshly mixed mortar to tool all the courses to an angled finish. Finally, fill the joints between the crazy paving with mortar and work to a peaked finish.

7 Selecting crazy paving
When selecting pieces of stone, place them together in different ways to achieve the best fit and reduce the need for cutting. Use the bricklayer's hammer to cut stone. Make a complete rectangle, the correct size for one tread, before mortaring.

Roman arch shrine

★ ★ ★
Advanced

Making time
One weekend
*One day for the base
slab and form, and
one day for building
the arch*

Many countries have an ancient tradition of building shrines in quiet corners of the house and garden, perhaps for religious purposes or for displaying a meaningful family item. This shrine has been inspired by the little arch-topped alcoves and niches common in Italy. It would be perfect for displaying a piece of garden sculpture or a favorite container plant, or it could comprise part of a water feature.

Considering the design

The arch is constructed over a wooden form set on wedges on the base slab, with its back against a wall. Stone is set in mortar over the form, the courses are jointed, and when the mortar has set, the wedges and form are removed. The rule of thumb is the thinner and more uniform the pieces of stone, the easier it is to run them over the arch.

Getting started

Start by building the form. It is very simple—just two sheets of plywood held apart with lengths of wood, and the sides of the shape covered in plywood.

Overall dimensions and general notes

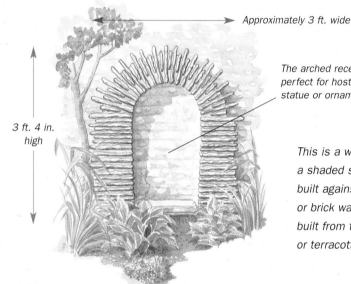

Approximately 3 ft. wide

The arched recess is perfect for hosting a statue or ornament

3 ft. 4 in. high

This is a wonderful project for a shaded site. It has to be built against an existing stone or brick wall. The arch can be built from thin stone, slate, or terracotta roof tiles.

You will need

Tools

✔ Tape measure, straightedge, and compass
✔ Crosscut saw
✔ Saber saw
✔ Claw hammer
✔ Screwdriver
✔ Pegs and string
✔ Spade and shovel
✔ Wheelbarrow and bucket
✔ Spirit level
✔ Sledgehammer
✔ Bricklayer's hammer
✔ Brick trowel
✔ Pointing trowel
✔ Pliers
✔ Soft-bristled brush

Materials

For an arch 3 ft. 4 in. high and 3 ft. wide

✔ Gravel or crushed stone: about 1 wheelbarrow load
✔ Stone base slab: approx. 3 ft. long, 12 in. wide, and 2 in thick, color and texture of your choice
✔ Stone plinth slab: approx. 16 in. long, 6 in. wide, and 3 in. thick, slightly bigger than the base of the form

✔ Roof slate: 2 wheelbarrow loads of thin slate, either salvaged or split
✔ Plywood: 2 pieces, 28 in. long, 16 in. wide, and ¾ in. thick; 1 piece, 6 ft. long, 8 in. wide and ¾ in. thick (form)
✔ Pine: 15 pieces, 8 in. long, 1⅜ in. wide, and ¾ in. thick (form joining strips and wedges)
✔ Mortar: 1 part (22 lb.) Portland cement, 1 part (22 lb.) lime, 2 parts (44 lb.) well-graded mortar sand
✔ Screws: 50 x 1-in.-long cross-headed screws (this allows extra)
✔ Nails: 50 x 1-in.-long flat-headed nails (this allows extra)
✔ Soft galvanized wire: 24 in.

Exploded view of the former for the Roman arch shrine

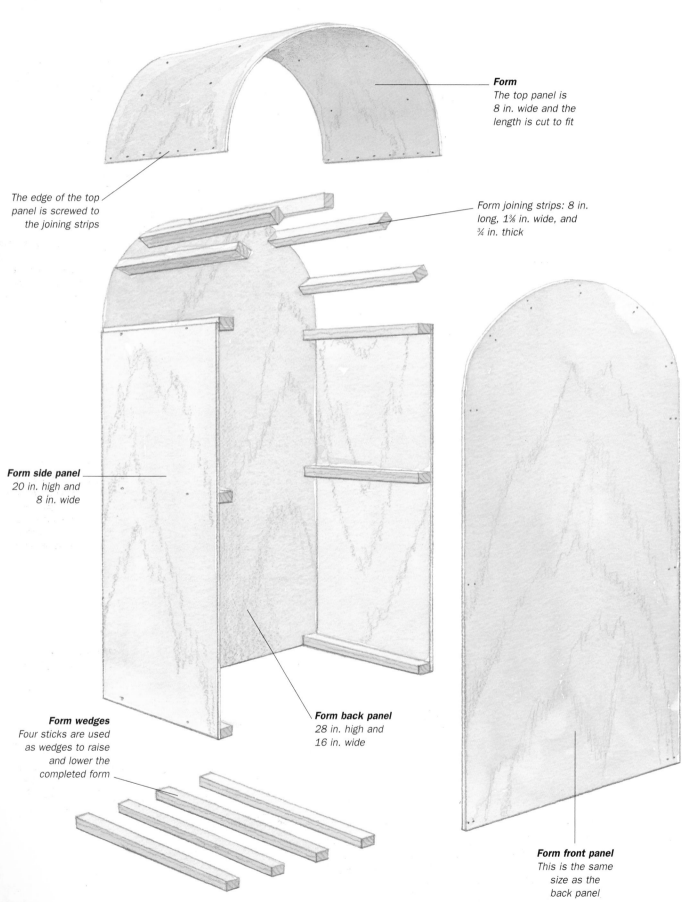

Form
The top panel is
8 in. wide and the
length is cut to fit

The edge of the top
panel is screwed to
the joining strips

Form joining strips: 8 in.
long, 1⅜ in. wide, and
¾ in. thick

Form side panel
20 in. high and
8 in. wide

Form wedges
Four sticks are used
as wedges to raise
and lower the
completed form

Form back panel
28 in. high and
16 in. wide

Form front panel
This is the same
size as the
back panel

Exploded view of the Roman arch shrine

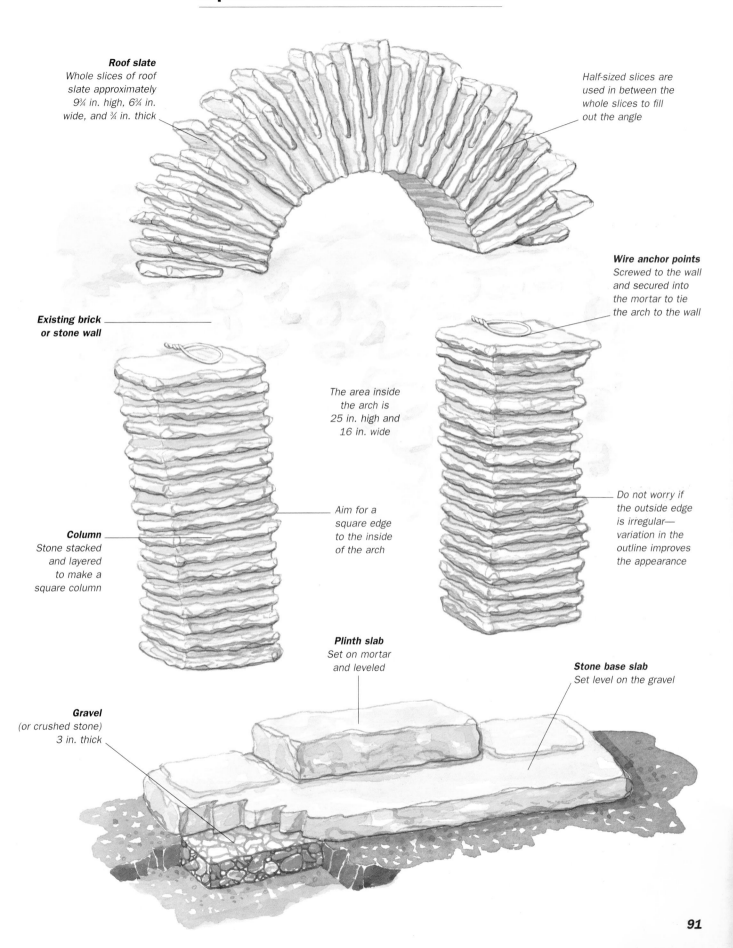

Roof slate
Whole slices of roof slate approximately 9¾ in. high, 6¾ in. wide, and ¾ in. thick

Half-sized slices are used in between the whole slices to fill out the angle

Wire anchor points
Screwed to the wall and secured into the mortar to tie the arch to the wall

Existing brick or stone wall

The area inside the arch is 25 in. high and 16 in. wide

Do not worry if the outside edge is irregular—variation in the outline improves the appearance

Aim for a square edge to the inside of the arch

Column
Stone stacked and layered to make a square column

Plinth slab
Set on mortar and leveled

Stone base slab
Set level on the gravel

Gravel
(or crushed stone) 3 in. thick

Making the Roman arch shrine

2 Covering the form
Cover the sides of the form with plywood. Ease the plywood over the curve, and screw it to the joining strips. Use a generous quantity of screws.

1 Making the form
Build the front and back of the form with the two sheets of plywood, setting them 8 in. apart, as shown in the working drawing. Nail or screw the plywood shapes directly to the ends of the 8-in.-long form joining strips.

3 Laying the base slab
Clear and level the site and compact the soil with the sledgehammer. Lay a 3 in. layer of gravel, and compact it with the sledgehammer. Set the base slab in place on generous blobs of mortar. Make checks with the spirit level.

4 Setting up the plinth slab
Bed the plinth slab in mortar on the base slab. Use the tape measure and spirit level to ensure that it is leveled and centered on the base slab.

5 Positioning the form

Place wedges of wood on the plinth and set the form on top of it, firmly against the wall. Make sure that it is leveled and centered. Pay particular attention to the side view, making sure that the form is not tilting forward (it can tilt backward slightly).

6 Building the arch

Mix the mortar to a butter-smooth consistency, and start to build layers of stone on each side of the form to make the square columns. Ensure that the stacks are both vertically and horizontally level by making regular checks with the spirit level.

7 Anchor wires

Screw twists of wire to the wall at four or five places around the top of the arch to provide anchor points for the stonework. As you build the columns, insert the ends of the wire into the mortar between the slices of stone to help hold the structure firm.

8 Forming the arch

Stack pieces of stone over the curved top of the form, setting half-slices between them to ensure a good spacing. Finally, when the mortar is dry and hard, use the pointing trowel to sculpt the mortar to reveal the edges of the stone.

Glossary

Back-filling

Filling a space that exists around a foundation or wall with soil.

Bedding

The process of setting (and leveling) a stone in a bed or layer of wet mortar.

Buttering

Using a trowel to spread a piece of stone with wet mortar, just prior to setting it in position—for example, in a wall.

Compacting

Using a hammer or other tool to squash down a layer of sand, soil, or gravel.

Coursing

Bedding a number of stones in mortar in order to build a horizontal course.

Curing time

The time necessary for mortar or concrete to become firm and stable. "Part cured" means that the mortar or concrete is solid enough to continue work.

Dressing

Using a hammer, chisel, or trowel to trim a stone to size; alternatively, to create a textured finish on its surface.

Dry run

Running through the procedure of setting out the components of a structure without using concrete, mortar, or another adhesive; or trying a technique in order to find out whether it will be successful.

Floating

Using a metal, plastic, or wooden float to skim wet concrete or mortar to a smooth and level finish.

Leveling

Using a spirit level to confirm whether or not a structure or stone is level, then going on to make adjustments to bring individual stones into line.

Marking out

Using string, pegs, and a tape measure to set out the size of a foundation on the ground; also, to mark out an individual stone in readiness for cutting.

Planning

The whole procedure of considering a project, viewing the site, making drawings, and working out amounts and costs prior to actually starting work.

Pointing

Using a trowel or a tool of your choice to fill, shape, and texture mortar joints.

Raking out

Using a trowel to rake out some mortar in a joint in order that the edges of a stone are more clearly revealed.

Sighting

To judge by eye, or to look down or along a wall, in order to determine whether or not a structure is level.

Siting

Making decisions as to where—in the yard or on the plot—a structure should be positioned.

Sourcing

The process of questioning suppliers by phone, visit, letter, or e-mail in order to ascertain the best source for materials.

Tamping

Using a length of wood to compact and level wet concrete.

Trimming

Using a hammer, chisel, the edge of large trowel, or a tool of your own choosing to improve the finish on the edge of a piece of stone. It is similar to Dressing (see above).

Watering or damping

Wetting a stone before bedding in on mortar to prevent the stone from sucking the water out of the mortar.

Wedging

Using small pieces of stone to wedge larger pieces of stone, so that they reach a desired level.

Wire brushing

Using a wire-bristled brush to remove dry mortar from the face of a stone.

Index

AG&G Books would like to
thank Garden and Wildlife
Matters Photographic Library
for contributing the photographs
used on pages 7 and 18–23.